CLASSICAL COMICS
TEACHING RESOURCE PACK

Making Shakespeare accessible
for teachers and students

Suitable for teaching ages 10-17

Written by: Ian McNeilly
US Adaptation: Joe Sutliff Sanders

Romeo & Juliet

CLASSICAL COMICS
TEACHING RESOURCE PACK
Romeo & Juliet

Perfect bound edition published 2013
First published 2009

Published by: Classical Comics
Copyright ©2009 Classical Comics Ltd.

Written by: Ian McNeilly
US Adaptation: Joe Sutliff Sanders
Character Designs & Original Artwork: Will Volley
Coloring: Jim Devlin
Design & Layout: Jo Wheeler & Jenny Placentino
Editor in Chief: Clive Bryant

The rights of Ian McNeilly, Will Volley, Jim Devlin and Joe Sutliff
Sanders to be identified as the artists of this work have been asserted
in accordance with the Copyright, Designs and Patents Act 1988
sections 77 and 78.

Acknowledgments: Every effort has been made to trace copyright
holders of material reproduced in this book. Any rights not
acknowledged here will be acknowledged in subsequent editions if
notice is given to Classical Comics Ltd.

All enquiries should be addressed to:
Classical Comics Ltd.
PO Box 16310
Birmingham
B30 9EL
United Kingdom

education@classicalcomics.com
www.classicalcomics.com

ISBN: 978-1-907127-74-8

Printed in the USA

CONTENTS

INTRODUCTION 6

BACKGROUND
William Shakespeare 7
Romeo and Juliet – Shakespeare's Story? 10
Famous Shakespeare Quotations 11

UNDERSTANDING THE PLAY
Act Summaries 13
Questions: Acts One to Five 18
Sequencing 23
Timeline 27
What Happens Next? 29
"Fate" or Just "Bad Luck"? 34

CHARACTER
Character Study: Romeo 36
Character Study: Juliet 37
Character Study: Mercutio 38
Character Study: Tybalt 39
Character Study: Paris 40
Character Study: Benvolio 41
Character Study: Nurse 42
Character Study: Friar Laurence 43
Character Study: Prince Escalus 44
Character Study: Lords and Ladies 45
Matching Quotations 46
Characters and Adjectives 48

LANGUAGE
Adjectives – Widening Your Vocabulary 49
Similes 50
Metaphors 51
Oxymorons 53
Juliet's Ambiguity 54
Missing Words 55
Close Textual Analysis 56

DRAMA AND DISCUSSION
Formal Debate 58
Playscript Writing and Performance – "The Scene Unseen" 60
Casting Director's Planning Notes 62
After the Deaths – The Inquest 64

CREATIVE WRITING
Juliet's "Suicide" Note 65
Character Diaries 66
The Verona News 67
Film Review 69
Verona Obituaries 70
Magazine Interview 72
A Modern Version of *Romeo and Juliet* 73

ESSAY WRITING 74

GAMES AND ACTIVITIES
Romeo and Juliet Spelling Jumble 76
Romeo and Juliet Word Search 77
Romeo and Juliet Crossword 78

TEACHERS' NOTES, ANSWERS AND EXPANSIONS 79

INTRODUCTION

WELCOME TO THE *ROMEO AND JULIET* TEACHING RESOURCE FROM CLASSICAL COMICS.

This teaching resource aims to provide enough information and inspiration to satisfy any teacher of this text, and to offer enjoyable and accessible activities. It is designed with ease of use in mind: it is easy to photocopy, and the accompanying disk means that not only can the activities be printed out directly, but they can also be displayed on a whiteboard for class study.

The activities are designed to suit students ranging from ages 10 to 17; and, to assist the busy teacher, they may be used with little or no preparation. Some are informative, some are worksheets, and some stimulate discussion and/or potentially substantial writing tasks.

This teaching resource can be used alongside the Classical Comics adaptation, although that definitely isn't a requirement – it works equally well with any traditional text.

Within these pages you will see opportunities for cross-curricular study including media studies, PSHE, drama, and art and design. As far as the English curriculum goes, careful selection of activities will ensure that many aspects of speaking and listening, reading and writing are covered – whichever grade is being taught.

I sincerely hope that this teaching resource is of great benefit to you and will in turn help your students to engage with and enjoy this wonderful play.

Ian McNeilly

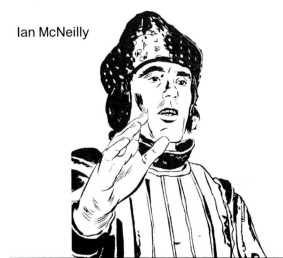

"Where be these enemies? Capulet! Montague!
See, what a scourge is laid upon your hate,
That heaven finds means to kill your joys with love!"
Prince Escalus, Act 5 Scene 3

Ian McNeilly has taught English in a variety of secondary schools and sixth forms both in the UK and overseas. He currently teaches part-time at Brantwood School in Sheffield, England. Ian, who holds a Masters degree in Literature Studies, has been Head of Department and an examiner for Cambridge International Examinations. He is also the Director for the National Association for the Teaching of English (NATE) – the professional body for all those working in English education. This role ensures his involvement with curriculum developments, and he is often called upon to comment on such matters in the English national press.

Website: www.nate.org.uk
Contact: director_nate@yahoo.co.uk

WILLIAM SHAKESPEARE C.1564 – 1616

Shakespeare is, without question, the world's most famous playwright. Yet, despite his fame, very few records and artifacts of him exist today. We don't even know the exact date of his birth! Traditionally, however, April 23rd 1564 (St George's Day) is taken to be his birthday, as this was three days before his baptism (for which we do have a record). Records also tell us that he died on the same date in 1616, aged fifty-two.

Jon Haward and Gary Erskine

The life of William Shakespeare can be divided into three acts.

Act One – Stratford-upon-Avon
William was the eldest son of tradesman John Shakespeare and Mary Arden, and the third of eight children (he had two older sisters). The Shakespeares were a respectable family. John made gloves and traded leather. The year after William was born, John became an alderman of Stratford-upon-Avon, and four years later he became High Bailiff (or mayor) of the town. Plague and illnesses were common in sixteenth-century England. The Bubonic Plague took the lives of many and was believed to have been the cause of death for three of William's seven siblings.

Little is known of William's childhood. He learned to read and write at the local primary school, and later he is believed to have attended the local grammar school, where he studied Latin and English Literature. In 1582, aged eighteen, William married a local farmer's daughter, Anne Hathaway. Anne was eight years his senior and three months pregnant. During their marriage they had three children: Susanna, born on May 26, 1583, and twins, Hamnet and Judith, born on February 2nd 1585. Hamnet, William's only son, died in 1596, aged eleven, from Bubonic Plague. Interestingly, the play *Hamlet* was written four years later.

Act Two – London
Five years into his marriage, in 1587, William's wife and children stayed in Stratford, while he moved to London. He appeared as an actor at "The Theatre" (England's first permanent theater), and gave public recitals of his own poems, but he quickly became famous for his playwriting. His fame soon spread far and wide. When Queen Elizabeth I died in 1603, the new King James I (who was already King James VI of Scotland) gave royal consent for Shakespeare's acting company, "The Lord Chamberlain's Men", to be called "The King's Men" in return for entertaining the court. This association was to shape a number of plays, such as *Macbeth*, which was written to please the Scottish King.

William Shakespeare is attributed with writing and collaborating on 38 plays, 154 sonnets and 5 poems, in just twenty-three years, between 1590 and 1613. No original manuscript exists for any of his plays, making it hard to date them accurately. Printing was still in its infancy, and plays tended to change as they were performed. Shakespeare would write manuscripts for the actors and continue to refine them over a number of performances. The plays we know today have survived from written copies taken at various stages of each play and usually written by the actors from memory. This has given rise to variations in texts of what is now known as "quarto" versions of the plays, until we reach the first official printing of each play in the 1623 "folio", *Mr William Shakespeare's Comedies, Histories, & Tragedies*.

In 1599, Shakespeare and his troupe built "The Globe Theatre" (using timbers from "The Theatre" that they carried by boat across the River Thames!). This theater, made even more famous today because of the "New Globe Theatre" on London's south bank, became the home of Shakespeare's plays, with thousands of people crammed into the small space for each performance. This lasted until 1613, when a cannon shot during a performance of *Henry VIII* set fire to the thatched roof and the entire theater burned to the ground. Although it was rebuilt a year later, it marked an end to Shakespeare's writing and to his time in London.

WILLIAM SHAKESPEARE C.1564 – 1616

Act Three - Retirement

Shakespeare returned to live with his family in Stratford-upon-Avon. His last documented visit to London was in 1614 – a business trip with his son-in-law John Hall. William Shakespeare died on April 23, 1616, and was buried two days later at the Church of the Holy Trinity (the same church where he had been baptized fifty-two years earlier). The cause of his death remains unknown.

His gravestone bears these words, believed to have been written by William himself:-

> *Good friend for Jesus sake forbear*
> *To dig the dust enclosed here.*
> *Blest be the man that spares these stones,*
> *And curst be he that moves my bones.*

Epilogue

At the time of his death, Shakespeare had substantial properties, which he bestowed on his family and associates from the theater. He had no son to inherit his wealth, and the fact that he wrote his second will in March 1616 displays an awareness of his likely death. His signature on that will is very shaky. The bulk of his will, including his substantial home, was left to his eldest daughter, Susanna. Susanna's husband, John Hall, was the executor of the will. To his other daughter, Judith, he left money and possessions. Curiously, the only thing that he left to his wife, Anne, was his second-best bed! (although she continued to live in the family home after his death). William Shakespeare's last direct descendant died in 1670. She was his granddaughter, Elizabeth.

TO BE, OR NOT TO BE – THAT IS THE QUESTION	True or False?
1. Shakespeare was born in Stratford-upon-Avon in 1564	
2. His life and times are well documented	
3. Shakespeare's family were very poor	
4. He never went to school	
5. William Shakespeare married Anne Hathaway	
6. The whole Shakespeare family moved to London in 1587	
7. Shakespeare's group of actors performed his plays for King James I	
8. Shakespeare died in London	
9. Shakespeare was buried in Stratford-upon-Avon in 1616	
10. Descendants of Shakespeare are still alive today	

WILLIAM SHAKESPEARE c.1564 – 1616
A (VERY) BRIEF BIOGRAPHY

Despite his fame, few records exist for the life of William Shakespeare. He was born in Stratford-upon-Avon, we believe on April 23, 1564. William was the eldest son of a respectable and reasonably affluent family. His father, John, was a local tradesman who went on to become the mayor of the town.

William learned to read and write at the local primary school, and later he is believed to have attended grammar school. When he was 18, he married a local farmer's daughter, Anne Hathaway. They had three children together.

Five years later, the family stayed in Stratford while he moved to London. He appeared as an actor and gave public recitals of his own poems, but he quickly became famous for his playwriting. His fame soon spread far and wide. When Queen Elizabeth I died in 1603, the new King James I (who was already King James VI of Scotland) gave royal consent for Shakespeare's acting company to be called "The King's Men" in return for entertaining the court. This association was to shape a number of plays, such as *Macbeth*, which was written to please the Scottish King.

William Shakespeare is attributed with writing and collaborating on 38 plays, 154 sonnets and 5 poems between around 1590 and 1613. No original manuscript exists for any of his plays, making it hard to date them accurately and impossible to decide upon a definitive version

In 1599, Shakespeare and his troupe built "The Globe Theatre." This theater became the home of Shakespeare's plays, with thousands of people crammed into the small space for each performance. In 1613, a cannon shot during a performance of *Henry VIII* set fire to the thatched roof, and the entire theater burned to the ground. Although it was rebuilt a year later, it marked an end to Shakespeare's writing and his time in London.

Shakespeare returned to Stratford-upon-Avon and died on April 23, 1616, aged 52. The cause of his death remains unknown. William Shakespeare's last direct descendant (his granddaughter, Elizabeth) died childless in 1670.

TO BE, OR NOT TO BE – THAT IS THE QUESTION

	True or False?
1. Shakespeare was born in Stratford-upon-Avon in 1564	
2. His life and times are well documented	
3. Shakespeare's family were very poor	
4. He never went to school	
5. William Shakespeare married Anne Hathaway	
6. The whole Shakespeare family moved to London in 1587	
7. Shakespeare's group of actors performed his plays for King James I	
8. Shakespeare died in London	
9. Shakespeare was buried in Stratford-upon-Avon in 1616	
10. Descendants of Shakespeare are still alive today	

ROMEO AND JULIET – SHAKESPEARE'S STORY?

Believe it or not, Shakespeare's talent did not lie in original storytelling. Most of the plots of his plays were stories that existed already in a variety of forms, whether as poems, prose, or events that actually happened in history, although he often changed all of these significantly.

Romeo and Juliet is no different. It was written relatively early in his career, when Shakespeare was in his early thirties (finished around 1595). It was first published in 1597, though that version was of poor quality and was later revised.

In many ways, the play is rooted in tradition. The theme of young lovers thwarted by events beyond their control is almost as ancient as storytelling itself, and some academics say it can be traced back as far as the birth of Christ, to Roman writer Ovid's "Pyramus and Thisbe", in which the parents hate each other and Pyramus wrongly believes his lover Thisbe is dead. There is also a clear link to a book from the third century AD and one of the earliest novels ever written, the "Ephesiaca" by ancient Greek writer Xenophon of Ephesus.

In the 1400s the tale became popular in Italy and France and was expanded to include more details, some of which can be recognized in Shakespeare's *Romeo and Juliet*. In 1562, two years before Shakespeare's birth, an English poet called Arthur Brooke composed a narrative poem called *The Tragicall History of Romeus and Juliet*, which was a translation of earlier Italian and French efforts.

Twenty years later in 1582, another English author called William Painter included a version of the story in his prose work *Palace of Pleasure*. The works of Brooke and Painter were used heavily by Shakespeare for his plot and some of his characterization.

One of the most often asked questions about *Romeo and Juliet* is "Is it a true story?" The answer is probably "no," though some true romantics believe to have evidence proving that it took place. It is true that in thirteenth-century Italy there were two very powerful rival families – the Montecchis and the Capellettis. The Montecchis even lived in Verona. But the Capellettis lived in Cremona which is over an hour away...by car!

It is definitely "true" in the sense that very similar things have happened to young people since the beginning of time – and are still happening today.

FAMOUS SHAKESPEARE QUOTATIONS

TASK:

Shakespeare is probably the most quoted writer in the history of English Literature. Here is a small selection of the wise words of William Shakespeare. What do you think the quotations mean?

WISE WORDS	YOUR INTERPRETATION:
"Out, out, brief candle! Life's but a walking shadow, a poor player, That struts and frets his hour upon the stage, And then is heard no more. It is a tale Told by an idiot, full of sound and fury, Signifying nothing." *Macbeth*	
"As flies to wanton boys are we to th' gods, They kill us for their sport." *King Lear*	
"Excellent wretch! Perdition catch my soul But I do love thee! and when I love thee not, Chaos is come again." *Othello*	
"Neither a borrower nor a lender be, For loan oft loses both itself and friend, And borrowing dulls the edge of husbandry." *Hamlet*	
"Uneasy lies the head that wears a crown." *Henry VI, Part II*	
"All the world's a stage, And all the men and women merely players; They have their exits and their entrances, And one man in his time plays many parts, His acts being seven ages." *As You Like It*	

FAMOUS SHAKESPEARE QUOTATIONS

WISE WORDS	YOUR INTERPRETATION:
"All that glisters is not gold." *The Merchant of Venice*	
"The course of true love never did run smooth;" *A Midsummer Night's Dream*	
"Cowards die many times before their deaths, The valiant never taste of death but once." *Julius Caesar*	
"Why then the world's mine oyster, Which I with sword will open." *The Merry Wives of Windsor*	
"The first thing we do, let's kill all the lawyers." *Henry VI*	
"Once more unto the breach, dear friends, once more; Or close the wall up with our English dead. In peace there's nothing so becomes a man As modest stillness and humility; But when the blast of war blows in our ears, Then imitate the action of the tiger...." *Henry V*	

ROMEO & JULIET - ACT SUMMARIES

ACT ONE

Scene 1   It is Sunday, and the streets of Verona are busy. Two Capulet servants, Sampson and Gregory, are teasing each other quite rudely and as early as the seventh line mention how much they hate a rival family, the Montagues. Abraham and Balthasar of the Montagues enter, and a fight breaks out. Benvolio tries to stop it, but Tybalt refuses to help, and the fight turns into a riot that is eventually broken up by the town guards. The Prince threatens death to anyone who disturbs the peace again. Romeo enters after the scene and tells his friend Benvolio that he wants nothing to do with violence. He also admits to being lovesick because the woman he loves (Rosaline) doesn't want to know him.

Scene 2   Paris visits Lord Capulet, asking to marry his daughter, Juliet. We learn she is not quite 14 years old, and Capulet tells Paris to wait two more years. Nevertheless, Capulet invites Paris to a masked ball, or party, at their house. Benvolio and Romeo find out about the party, and Benvolio encourages Romeo to go so that he can forget about Rosaline.

Scene 3   Lady Capulet tells Juliet that Paris wants to marry her. Juliet's Nurse is very excited, but Juliet hasn't thought about marriage yet.

Scene 4   It's now Sunday evening, and several partygoers, among them Romeo, Benvolio and Mercutio, are outside Capulet's house. Mercutio's light-hearted and clever banter contrasts with Romeo's dark mood, though it's obvious Mercutio has his own dark side too.

Scene 5   Preparations are being made for Capulet's party, and the guests arrive, followed by lots of dancing and music. Romeo sees Juliet for the first time, from a distance, and is overwhelmed by her beauty. Despite his mask, Romeo (Montague) is spotted by Tybalt (Capulet), who wants to kill Romeo for sneaking in uninvited – but Capulet forcefully stops him. Tybalt is angered by this and vows revenge against Romeo. Romeo approaches Juliet. They talk and then kiss. Nurse interrupts and tells Romeo that Juliet is a Capulet, much to his dismay. Later, Juliet finds out that Romeo is a Montague, and she reacts in much the same way.

ROMEO & JULIET - ACT SUMMARIES

ACT TWO

Scene 1	Romeo manages to hide from his friends outside Capulet's orchard and refuses to join them, despite Mercutio's teasing.
Scene 2	This is perhaps the most famous scene in the history of English drama, known as "The Balcony Scene." Romeo is in the orchard and sees Juliet high on her balcony. Not knowing Romeo is there, Juliet speaks about him lovingly but laments the fact that he's a Montague. Romeo lets her know that he is there. Juliet is shocked, but the two of them engage in loving conversation. Again interrupted by the Nurse, they hastily arrange to marry.
Scene 3	It is now early on Monday morning, and Romeo goes to see his friend, Friar Laurence. When Laurence last saw Romeo he was lovesick about Rosaline, and Laurence is pleased to see the change in him – until he realizes that Romeo wants to marry some new girl. Friar Laurence agrees to marry Romeo to Juliet in the hope that the union will bring peace to the warring families.
Scene 4	This is a very happy scene and the only one in the play in which we see Romeo enjoying time with his friends. Mercutio teases Benvolio and Romeo. The Nurse arrives, and Mercutio teases her mercilessly, provoking her anger. Romeo tells the Nurse to inform Juliet that she should go to Friar Laurence's cell that afternoon to be married.

Scene 5	Juliet anxiously awaits the Nurse's return. When she does come back, she takes a long time to reveal the message, much to the annoyance of Juliet.
Scene 6	Romeo waits for Juliet with Friar Laurence. She arrives, and the couple kiss. Romeo and Juliet are married – though, interestingly, the ceremony is not performed on stage.

ROMEO & JULIET - ACT SUMMARIES

ACT THREE

Scene 1	This is the play's pivotal scene. The audience (and Romeo, of course!) will be on an emotional high after the wedding, but it all comes crashing down in this scene. It is only one hour after the marriage. Benvolio and Mercutio talk in Verona's streets. Benvolio is trying to persuade Mercutio to go indoors as it is very hot and he fears a brawl if they come across the Capulets. Typically, Mercutio rejects this idea and teases Benvolio. Tybalt enters; he and Mercutio have a heated discussion. Romeo enters. Tybalt hands out insults to Romeo, who does not take the bait. Instead, Mercutio fights Tybalt, and is killed; Tybalt strikes the fatal blow as Romeo moves between them. Grief-stricken, feeling guilty and seeking revenge, Romeo kills Tybalt. He runs away, and the Prince, in Romeo's absence, banishes him from Verona.
Scene 2	Juliet has no idea what has gone on and sits at home looking forward to her wedding night with Romeo. The Nurse enters, crying, shouting Romeo's name and that someone has died. Juliet assumes it is Romeo but soon discovers it is Tybalt – and that Romeo killed him. At first she criticizes Romeo; then, she defends him to the Nurse. The Nurse agrees to find Romeo, telling him to come and bid farewell to Juliet.
Scene 3	We return to Friar Laurence's cell, where Romeo is understandably distraught by events. Laurence tries to make him see sense, but Romeo won't hear it. The Nurse enters and tells Romeo that Juliet is constantly crying. Romeo takes a knife and offers to stab himself to remove his name. Friar Laurence stops him, and becomes angry. Laurence tells Romeo to visit Juliet as previously arranged but warns him to make sure he leaves Verona before dawn and go to nearby Mantua.
Scene 4	It is late on Monday evening, and Paris has visited Capulet to repeat his request to marry Juliet. Capulet changes his mind, as he thinks it will cheer her up following the death of her cousin, and sets Thursday as the wedding day.
Scene 5	It is now very early on Tuesday morning, in Juliet's bedroom. Romeo and Juliet have spent the night together, and neither wants to part, although they realize Romeo must go or risk death if he is captured. Romeo leaves. Lady Capulet enters and tells Juliet that she will be married to Paris on Thursday. Juliet refuses. Lord Capulet becomes very angry and threatens her. Juliet turns to the Nurse, but her advice is to marry Paris. Juliet, realizing she has nowhere else to turn, plans to visit Friar Laurence for help.

ROMEO & JULIET - ACT SUMMARIES

ACT FOUR

Scene 1	Paris is with Friar Laurence, trying to arrange his marriage to Juliet, when she enters. Paris leaves, and Juliet threatens to kill herself if Laurence cannot help her. He comes up with a plan: she should go home and tell her father that she is sorry and will marry Paris. Laurence provides Juliet with a potion that will make her unconscious, mimicking the signs of death for 42 hours. She will then be taken to the Capulet tomb and laid to rest. In the meantime, the Friar will send a message to Romeo, telling him to return secretly from Mantua and take Juliet away once she wakes up.
Scene 2	It is now Tuesday afternoon and the Capulet household is preparing for the wedding. Juliet enters and apologizes to her father. Capulet decides to move the wedding forward by a day to Wednesday (the very next day).
Scene 3	Juliet is in her bedroom with the Nurse and her mother but manages to get them to leave, as this is necessary for her plan to work. Juliet is very worried about the potential consequences of drinking the potion; but, finally, she does it.
Scene 4	Wednesday morning in the Capulet house, and wedding preparations are in full swing.
Scene 5	The Nurse goes to Juliet's bedroom to wake her up but realizes she is "dead." The scene is one of great emotion (and also dramatic irony, seeing as the audience knows that she is still alive) as the Nurse, Lord and Lady Capulet and Paris all grieve over the shocking event. Friar Laurence enters and tries to reassure everyone that she will be peaceful and happy now. Capulet says all the preparations for a wedding will now change to a funeral.

ROMEO & JULIET - ACT SUMMARIES

ACT FIVE

Scene 1   The setting switches to Romeo in exile in Mantua. His servant Balthasar has gone on horseback to see him and inform him that Juliet has died, her body placed in Capulet's family tomb. Romeo asks Balthasar if he is carrying any message from the Friar, but he has none. Romeo plans to return to Verona and see Juliet. He plans to kill himself and lay with her in the vault. He stops off on the way and buys some very strong poison with which to kill himself.

Scene 2   We discover that Friar Laurence had previously sent Friar John to deliver a letter to Romeo in Mantua. However, Friar John returns, explaining he was unable to do so. He wasn't even allowed to leave Verona by the city's health officers, as he was suspected of carrying an illness. Immediately realizing the potentially disastrous consequences of this, Laurence asks Friar John to get him a crow bar. Juliet will awake shortly, and the Friar intends to break into the tomb to be with her. He plans to keep her at his cell until he can inform Romeo about what has happened.

Scene 3   Paris has gone to Juliet's tomb to pay his respects. Romeo also approaches the tomb. Not knowing anything about the relationship between Romeo and Juliet, Paris assumes that Romeo has come to do something vile against the Capulets, seeing as he is a Montague. Paris challenges Romeo, who tries to warn him not to do so. Paris rejects this advice, the pair fight, and Paris is killed. Romeo, not realizing that Juliet will shortly awake, is surprised at how her cheeks and lips have kept their color. Overwhelmed by grief, he drinks the poison, gives Juliet a final kiss and dies. Friar Laurence enters the tomb, and Juliet wakes. Some noise from outside signifies that they are about to be disturbed, most likely by the Watch. Fearing capture, Laurence runs away. Juliet stays. Realizing Romeo has killed himself with poison, she tries to do the same, but there isn't any left. She kisses Romeo, then stabs herself with his dagger. The Watch and the Prince enter, as do Lord and Lady Capulet and Lord Montague. We find out that Lady Montague died earlier that night, heartbroken at Romeo's exile. Friar Laurence and Balthasar are captured by the Watch. Laurence later tells the whole story to the Prince, who believes him, especially as he is supported by a letter in Romeo's own hand, given to the Prince by Balthasar. A saddened and enraged Prince condemns the hatred between the two families. Capulet and Montague shake hands; the pair say that they will build golden statutes of Romeo and Juliet to remind the people of Verona the power of true love and the need to live peacefully.

QUESTIONS – ACT ONE

COSY CAPULETS

1. Which of the servants bites his thumb? (Scene 1)

2. How old is Juliet? (Scene 2)

3. Whom does Lady Capulet want Juliet to marry? (Scene 3)

4. Who is Queen Mab? (Scene 4)

5. How many times do Romeo and Juliet kiss? (Scene 5)

MIND-BENDING MONTAGUES

1. How does Shakespeare immediately introduce Tybalt as a menacing character? Look closely at the language. (Scene 1)

2. How does Shakespeare create an immediate mood of sadness around Romeo? Again, look closely at the language. (Scene 1)

3. How does Paris try to convince Capulet that Juliet isn't too young to be married? Were you surprised by this? (Scene 2)

4. Explain why the Nurse and Juliet have a particularly close relationship. (Scene 3)

5. Why do you think Shakespeare chose to have Romeo and Juliet use religious vocabulary when they first meet? (Scene 5)

QUESTIONS – ACT TWO

COSY CAPULETS

1. The word "balcony" is mentioned nowhere in this scene. Why do you think it has become known as "The Balcony Scene"? (Scene 2)

2. With whom does Friar Laurence think Romeo has been spending time? (Scene 3)

3. Romeo tells the Nurse the marriage arrangements. Where should Juliet go, and when? (Scene 4)

4. The Nurse left Juliet at 9 o'clock. What time does she return with the message? (Scene 5)

5. What excuse is Juliet going to invent in order to get out of her house? (Scene 5)

MIND-BENDING MONTAGUES

1. Why is Romeo's description of Juliet as "the sun" a particularly good metaphor? (Scene 2)

2. Why does Juliet not want Romeo to swear by the moon? (Scene 2)

3. Why does Friar Laurence agree to marry Romeo and Juliet? What do you think of his idea? (Scene 3)

4. How is Tybalt's character developed in Scene 4...even though he isn't in it?

5. Explain how the Nurse, on her return from seeing Romeo, annoys Juliet. (Scene 5)

QUESTIONS – ACT THREE

COSY CAPULETS

1.   What does Mercutio tease Benvolio about? (Scene 1)

2.   Why does Mercutio fight with Tybalt? (Scene 1)

3.   At first, who does Juliet think has been killed when she meets the Nurse? (Scene 2)

4.   What does Capulet change his mind about in Scene 4?

5.   Where is Romeo going, after he leaves Juliet? (Scene 5)

MIND-BENDING MONTAGUES

1.   Does Benvolio tell the truth in his account of the fighting? Explain your answer. (Scene 1)

2.   Explain why Romeo thinks banishment is a punishment worse than death. (Scene 3)

3.   Why should Romeo be happy, according to Friar Laurence? (Scene 3)

4.   In Scene 4, Capulet tells Paris he only wants a small wedding ceremony. Why?

5.   Explain Romeo and Juliet's reference to larks and nightingales. (Scene 5)

QUESTIONS – ACT FOUR

COSY CAPULETS

1. What does Paris call Juliet, which she objects to?
    (Scene 1)

2. If the potion works as Friar Laurence hopes, for how long will
    Juliet be unconscious? (Scene 1)

3. Why does Juliet want to get the Nurse and her mother out of
    her room? (Scene 3)

4. When Juliet is found dead in her room on the morning of her
    wedding day, whom does Capulet say that she has married?
    (Scene 5)

5. How does Friar Laurence try to reassure the Capulet family?
    (Scene 5)

MIND-BENDING MONTAGUES

1. How does Juliet's conversation with Paris reveal a new dimension to her character?
    (Scene 1)

2. Work through Friar Laurence's plan, step-by-step. Do you think it is a good plan? Explain your answer.
    (Scene 1)

3. Juliet explains her fears in Scene 3. What are they?

4. List some simple language techniques that Shakespeare uses to emphasize the shock and grief the
    characters feel at Juliet's "death." (Scene 4)

5. What is your reaction to Friar Laurence's speech, which begins "Peace ho, for shame!"
    (Hint – think of "dramatic irony"). (Scene 5)

QUESTIONS – ACT FOUR

COSY CAPULETS

1. Why has Balthasar traveled to Mantua? (Scene 1)

2. How does Romeo persuade the Apothecary to sell him some poison? (Scene 1)

3. What critical piece of news does Friar Laurence hear from Friar John? (Scene 2)

4. When Romeo looks at the "dead" Juliet, what surprises him? (Scene 3)

5. The Prince says that he himself has lost two kinsmen. To whom is he referring? (Scene 3)

MIND-BENDING MONTAGUES

1. What conclusion do you think Romeo has reached when he says "Is it e'en so? then I defy you, stars!"
    (Scene 1)

2. Why is it important to the plot that Romeo uses a very strong poison, one which "if you had the
    strength/Of twenty men, it would dispatch you straight"? (Scene 1)

3. Do you have sympathy for Paris? Explain your answer. (Scene 3)

4. One of the biggest examples of dramatic irony in the whole
    of Shakespeare's works is when Romeo says, "Death, that
    hath suck'd the honey of thy breath,/Hath had no power yet
    upon thy beauty:/Thou art not conquer'd." Explain the
    dramatic irony. How did you feel as a reader/audience
    member at this point? (Scene 3)

5. Do you agree with Prince Escalus' conclusion that "All are
    punish'd"? Explain your views. (Scene 3)

SEQUENCING I

THE PROLOGUE

TASK:

The lines from the Prologue have all been mixed up! Can you put them in the right order? (Hint – there is a rhyme scheme…it's a b a b – except for the last two lines, which rhyme with each other!).

1　　From ancient grudge break to new mutiny,
　　　Where civil blood makes civil hands unclean.

2　　Whose misadventur'd piteous overthrows
　　　Doth with their death bury their parents' strife.

3　　The which if you with patient ears attend,
　　　What here shall miss, our toil shall strive to mend.

4　　Which, but their children's end, nought could remove,
　　　Is now the two hours' traffic of our stage;

5　　Two households, both alike in dignity,
　　　In fair Verona, where we lay our scene,

6　　From forth the fatal loins of these two foes
　　　A pair of star-cross'd lovers take their life;

7　　The fearful passage of their death-mark'd love,
　　　And the continuance of their parents' rage,

SEQUENCING I

UPDATE THE PROLOGUE

A "prologue" is something that comes at the beginning of a play (and sometimes stories and long, narrative poems), often giving information about events that have happened before the time the play itself begins. This is partly true in the case of *Romeo and Juliet*. However, Shakespeare goes much further, telling the audience key parts of what they are about to see – including the fact that the two lovers die! The language in the Prologue is varied in that some is very straightforward, whereas other parts are more complex.

TASK:

Your task is to move the language forward 400 years or so and write a modern Prologue which gives all the information Shakespeare wanted the audience to have. And no – it doesn't have to have a rhyming scheme!

Shakespeare's 16c. version	Your 21c. version
Two households, both alike in dignity, In fair Verona, where we lay our scene,	
From ancient grudge break to new mutiny, Where civil blood makes civil hands unclean.	
From forth the fatal loins of these two foes A pair of star-cross'd lovers take their life;	
Whose misadventur'd piteous overthrows Doth with their death bury their parents' strife.	
The fearful passage of their death-mark'd love, And the continuance of their parents' rage,	
Which, but their children's end, nought could remove, Is now the two hours' traffic of our stage;	
The which if you with patient ears attend; What here shall miss, our toil shall strive to mend.	

SEQUENCING II

THE PLAY – THIS ONE'S TOUGHER THAN TYBALT!

TASK:

The events in the play have been jumbled up! Cut them out and rearrange them into the order they appear in the play.

1. Romeo is banished from Verona by Prince Escalus.

2. Paris visits the Capulets' tomb.

3. Romeo and Juliet decide to get married.

4. Lady Capulet tells Juliet that Paris wants to marry her.

5. Juliet drinks a potion that will give her death-like symptoms.

6. Friar Laurence explains everything to Prince Escalus.

7. Juliet is told she has to marry Paris.

8. Tybalt kills Mercutio.

9. Friar Laurence enters the Capulets' tomb.

10. Romeo and Juliet kiss for the first time.

11. Romeo leaves Verona to go to Mantua.

12. Romeo tells Benvolio he is lovesick.

13. Romeo buys some very strong poison from an Apothecary.

14. Lord Montague says that his wife, Romeo's mother, has died of grief because of her son's exile.

15. Capulet and Montague shake hands and agree to build statues of their children.

16. Capulets and Montagues openly fight in a public place, though Romeo isn't present.

17. The wedding night of Romeo and Juliet.

18. Romeo sneaks into the Capulet orchard to see Juliet.

19. Romeo kills Paris.

20. Juliet kills herself with Romeo's dagger.

SEQUENCING II

21. Romeo and Juliet discover they are from rival families.

22. Juliet wakes up from her unconscious state.

23. Paris and Juliet have an awkward conversation.

24. Mercutio and Benvolio discuss Tybalt and his challenge to Romeo.

25. Balthasar visits Romeo in Mantua.

26. Friar Laurence agrees to marry Romeo and Juliet.

27. Capulet accepts Paris's offer to marry Juliet.

28. Friar Laurence leaves the Capulets' tomb.

29. The Nurse gets a message from Romeo, telling Juliet when the marriage will be.

30. Prince Escalus is angry with Capulet and Montague and says, "All are punish'd."

31. Juliet seeks the help of both her mother and the Nurse, but she is rejected.

32. Friar Laurence reveals a plan to help Juliet.

33. Romeo and Juliet meet at a party held at the Capulet house.

34. Hiding in Friar Laurence's cell, Romeo is stopped from stabbing himself.

35. Romeo and Juliet are married.

36. Romeo drinks the poison, kisses Juliet and dies.

37. Romeo kills Tybalt.

38. Friar John tells Friar Laurence that he failed to deliver his letter to Romeo.

39. Juliet is discovered "dead" in her chamber and taken to the Capulets' tomb.

40. Paris asks Capulet if he can marry Juliet, but he is refused.

TIMELINE

Romeo and Juliet sets a fast pace right from the public brawl in Act 1 Scene 1… and things just get faster and faster!

Shakespeare cranks up the speed throughout the play, until several characters are under so much pressure that they reach a breaking point.

Let's look at the character of Romeo. It's hard to believe but… Romeo is lovesick, falls in love with someone else, is married, has his wedding night, sees his best friend killed, murders his cousin (by marriage), is exiled, kills someone else, and then kills himself – all within the space of **FIVE DAYS**! Shakespeare makes even the fastest moving soap operas of today look positively tame.

The events come so rapidly that it is often very difficult to keep track of the passage of time in the play, even though Shakespeare makes several references to help us.

Here's a chronology:

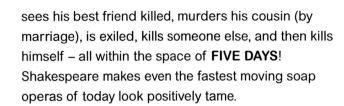

Sunday

9A.M.
The public brawl in Verona.

Midday
The invitations to Capulet's party are issued.

Afternoon
Juliet is told that Paris wants to marry her.

Evening
Romeo, Mercutio, Benvolio and others make their way to the party.

Night
Romeo and Juliet meet at the party.

Late night
Romeo manages to slip away from his friends.

Very late night/early Monday morning
"The Balcony Scene" in Juliet's orchard.

Monday

Early Monday morning
Romeo visits Friar Laurence, asking if the friar would marry him to Juliet.

9A.M.
Juliet sends the Nurse to give Romeo a message.

12P.M.
Nurse returns to Juliet with Romeo's message about the marriage arrangements.

Afternoon
Romeo and Juliet are married (less than a day after they met!).

An hour later
Tybalt kills Mercutio; Romeo kills Tybalt and is exiled.

Two hours after the killings
Juliet sends the Nurse to find Romeo.

Late evening
Capulet agrees to the marriage of Paris and Juliet, planned for Thursday.

Night
Romeo and Juliet spend their wedding night together.

TIMELINE

Tuesday

Very early morning
Romeo leaves Juliet to travel to Mantua.

Morning
Juliet is told she has to marry Paris.

Later morning
Juliet visits Friar Laurence, sees Paris there, and receives the potion.

Afternoon
Juliet apologizes to her father; he moves the wedding forward a day, to Wednesday.

Night
Juliet takes the potion.

Wednesday

Early morning
Juliet is found "dead."

Morning
Balthasar tells Romeo that Juliet is dead.

Afternoon/Evening
Friar Laurence finds out that Romeo has not received his letter.

Night/Late night
At the Capulet tomb, Romeo kills Paris, and then kills himself. Friar Laurence goes to the tomb and is there when Juliet wakes, but he leaves when he hears people approaching. She won't leave with him. Instead, she kills herself.

Thursday

Very early morning
Bodies are discovered (the Captain of the Watch says Juliet "hath lain this two days buried" so it must be Thursday), and the families are united.

WHAT HAPPENS NEXT?

TASK 1:

Look closely at the pictures on each card in the following pages. In the box, write down what you think is happening in each scene. You need to have read the play first!

Comic Card	WHAT IS HAPPENING? Describe in your own words. Try to explain what is going on in each panel and what the characters are saying. Can you remember what happens next?
CARD 1	
CARD 2	
CARD 3	
CARD 4	

COMIC CARD 1

Romeo & Juliet Act 1 Scene 1

COMIC CARD 2

Romeo & Juliet Act 2 Scene 2

COMIC CARD 3

Romeo & Juliet Act 3 Scene 1

COMIC CARD 4

Romeo & Juliet Act 4 Scene 5

"FATE" OR JUST "BAD LUCK"?

Put very simply, "fate" is a belief that things are destined to happen, that people's decisions and actions cannot ultimately change events.

"Bad luck" leads to unfortunate events, but often, with only a slight change in circumstances, these can be avoided.

Even more simply:

If it's fated, it's going to happen anyway, eventually.

Bad luck can change, and therefore so can final outcomes.

Some people believe that Romeo and Juliet were "fated" to meet, fall in love and have a tragic ending – there was nothing they could have done to change this. Another expression for fate in these circumstances is that "it was their destiny."

It is a theme that runs through many works, right from Ancient Greek literature to the present day. Take the Oscar-winning film *Slumdog Millionaire* for example. Although many seemingly impossible obstacles are placed in the way of the relationship between Jamal and Latika, they eventually get together because "it was written" – meaning it was their destiny, or fate. In that example, the ending is very uplifting; but this is not the case with *Romeo and Juliet*!

There is evidence in the play that Shakespeare wanted his audience to believe that fate was ruling their lives, thereby creating even more sympathy for the characters:

• Romeo and Juliet are described in the Prologue as "star-cross'd lovers" meaning that fate was against them.

• When entering the party, Romeo says, "my mind misgives/Some consequence, yet hanging in the stars,/Shall bitterly begin his fearful date/With this night's revels" (Act 1 Scene 4).

• After Romeo has killed Tybalt, he says, "O, I am fortune's fool!" (Act 3 Scene 1) meaning that he feels he is the plaything of fate/fortune.

• When Balthasar tells him that Juliet is dead, Romeo decides to fight against fate, which he feels is trying to prevent him from being with Juliet. He says, "then I defy you, stars!" meaning that he will take matters into his own hands by killing himself so that he can be with Juliet, even if it is in death.

• Just before Romeo drinks the poison, he says that he is about to "shake the yoke of inauspicious stars," which means that he will finally break free from the restrictions put upon him by fate.

"FATE" OR JUST "BAD LUCK"?

Those who don't believe in fate simply believe that Romeo and Juliet paid a heavy price for a series of very unlucky events – which makes it even more tragic when you think about it, as it opens up the possibility that Romeo and Juliet could have lived happily ever after. This heightened tragedy can be avoided from consideration if we believe in fate alone.

Which view do you take?

Were Romeo and Juliet victims of fate, thereby always destined for a tragic ending?

Or were they simply victims of bad luck, which could have been avoided?

Consider how the events of the play (and therefore the lives of Romeo and Juliet) would change if…

1.   Romeo had not killed Tybalt.

2.   Juliet had not been ordered to marry Paris.

3.   Balthasar had not seen Juliet "buried."

4.   Friar Laurence's letter had reached Romeo.

5.   Juliet had woken up five minutes earlier than she did.

ROMEO

Unlike Juliet, Romeo's age is not given; but one would imagine him to be a young, idealistic, romantic man between 16 and 19 years old – still a teenager, in other words. He begins the play "in love" with Rosaline but immediately forgets her when he sees someone more attractive, thus indicating his immaturity.

He is incredibly passionate, as can be seen in his whirlwind courtship of Juliet. He is not a naturally violent or argumentative person, judging from his reaction to the riot that opens the play and his initial refusal to fight Tybalt.

However, he is also very loyal, and when his best friend, Mercutio, is killed (partly because Romeo steps between them), his tender thoughts for Juliet are discarded, and his only thought is revenge, which he takes swiftly.

He is devastated at the news that he is to be exiled from Verona, reflecting the raw emotion of the young lover. This is writ large when he discovers Juliet is "dead." One can argue Romeo is immature and naive, but one can never argue that he isn't passionate or serious about Juliet – as his suicide reveals.

Important quotations by Romeo

"Did my heart love till now? forswear it, sight!
For I ne'er saw true beauty till this night."
(Act 1 Scene 5)

"But, soft! what light through yonder window
breaks?
It is the east, and Juliet is the sun!"
(Act 2 Scene 2)

"O, I am fortune's fool!"
(Act 3 Scene 1)

"There is no world without Verona walls;"
(Act 3 Scene 3)

"Is it e'en so? then I defy you, stars!"
(Act 5 Scene 1)

"Here's to my love! O true apothecary!
Thy drugs are quick. Thus with a kiss I die."
(Act 5 Scene 3)

TASK:
In the play, Romeo spends a day on his own in Mantua. Imagine he decides to compose a letter to Juliet, in which he includes an explanation of what happened in the fight, his feelings for her, and his future hopes and plans for them both. Write the letter.

JULIET

Most people, especially those who have seen the play in a theater or on film, are surprised when they find out that Juliet is two weeks short of her 14th birthday. She is "girlish" but sometimes seems mature for those tender years, and one must also remember that the play is set more than 400 years ago, when society and culture were very different. Remarkably, Paris points out that there are many happy mothers in Verona younger than Juliet.

When her mother puts it to her that Paris wants to marry her, she doesn't exhibit any girlish signs of excited enthusiasm. She is more reserved than both her mother and the Nurse. Perhaps the mention of love and marriage is still in her mind when she meets Romeo. She is completely won over by his bold romantic language (and actions!). Before meeting Romeo, she seems rather quiet and accepting of her status – but this rapidly changes. It is she, not Romeo, who is first to suggest marriage.

Juliet's language develops during the play, as can be seen in her conversations with Paris and her mother. She is too loyal to criticize Romeo or encourage Paris and the things she says are full of double meanings, displaying wit. Because of her fierce loyalty to Romeo, she condemns Tybalt and becomes angry with the Nurse when she criticizes him. Juliet's increasing maturity is also reflected by her standing up to her father (albeit temporarily).

She is a strong character, one who is emotionally abandoned by her family and physically abandoned by Romeo in exile. She is on her own when she takes a huge risk in drinking the potion. Like Romeo, her sincerity of feeling cannot be questioned – the brutality of the manner in which she takes her own life proves it.

Important quotations by Juliet

"My only love sprung from my only hate!"
(Act 1 Scene 5)

"O Romeo, Romeo! wherefore art thou Romeo?"
(Act 2 Scene 2)

"What's in a name? That which we call a rose,
By any other word would smell as sweet;"
(Act 2 Scene 2)

"Now, by Saint Peter's Church, and Peter too,
He shall not make me there a joyful bride."
(Act 3 Scene 5)

"O churl! drunk all, and left no friendly drop
To help me after?" (Act 5 Scene 3)

"Yea, noise? Then I'll be brief. O happy dagger!
This is thy sheath; there rust, and let me die."
(Act 5 Scene 3)

TASK:

For the boys – Would you like Juliet as a girlfriend?
For the girls – If Juliet was in your school, would you be friends with her?
Explain your answers!

MERCUTIO

Mercutio is Romeo's best friend and very popular among the Montague family. It should be remembered that he isn't a member of the family – in fact, he is a kinsman of Prince Escalus and therefore of very high social status.

You will see from the quotations below that he says a lot of noteworthy things in Act 3 Scene 1 – the scene in which both he and Tybalt die. If you didn't know the play, you might think that he doesn't say much before this. Nothing could be further from the truth. Every time Mercutio is on stage, he talks – a lot! He is very good at it, very creative and often magical with his language (see his "Queen Mab" speech in Act 1 Scene 4). Also, he is regularly very coarse and rude: qualities that would have appealed to the more bawdy members of Shakespeare's audience.

Mercutio is witty, vivacious, engaging, gregarious, and charming – but don't mistake him for a lightweight. He is a good friend to Romeo and has a deep sense of masculine honor which is why he is more than prepared to take up Tybalt's challenge, even if Romeo isn't.

Mercutio's death comes as a saddening shock not just for the Montagues, but also for the audience. We feel some of Romeo's loss because Mercutio is such a force on stage. In turn, this allows us to feel great sympathy and understanding for Romeo when he kills Tybalt.

Important quotations by Mercutio

"And but one word with one of us? couple it with something; make it a word and a blow."
(Act 3 Scene 1)

"Consort? what! dost thou make us minstrels?"
(Act 3 Scene 1)

"O calm, dishonourable, vile submission!"
(Act 3 Scene 1)

"Ask for me to-morrow,
and you shall find me a grave man." (Act 3 Scene 1)

"A plague o' both your houses!" (Act 3 Scene 1)

TASK:

As Verona was a violent place and Mercutio a rich man, suppose he had been encouraged by his lawyer to make a last will and testament.

Imagine that you are the lawyer who has to deal with his estate after his death.

What did Mercutio leave to people in his will? It's unlikely to have been straightforward, and there might even have been some funny conditions in there! Write the will.

TYBALT

Tybalt's influence on the play is huge, even though he doesn't speak that much (fewer than 40 lines in the whole play, believe it or not).

In Tybalt, Shakespeare creates a character that was very traditional at the time, playing the role of the "choleric" – a man who was prone to violence, aggression and mood swings.

Both Mercutio and Tybalt have a sense of honor; Mercutio only engages it when it is genuinely compromised, whereas Tybalt needs little valid excuse (Act 1 Scene 1, Act 1 Scene 5 and again in Act 3 Scene 1).

His character is developed in his absence (Act 2 Scene 4) when Mercutio and Benvolio talk of a challenge to Romeo that Tybalt has sent to Romeo's house. Tybalt is described as a man not to be messed with, one who knows what to do in a sword fight.

He exudes menace whenever he is on stage. The thing is, it's all pointless. His character is very similar to how some young people act today – his first resort is violence because he doesn't understand what "honor" really is. Tybalt confuses honor with his own reputation.

He ends up killing a decent man just before he needlessly loses his own life.

Important quotations by Tybalt

"What! art thou drawn among these heartless hinds?
Turn thee, Benvolio; look upon thy death."
(Act 1 Scene 1)

"This, by his voice, should be a Montague.
Fetch me my rapier, boy." (Act 1 Scene 5)

"It fits, when such a villain is a guest.
I'll not endure him." (Act 1 Scene 5)

"Boy, this shall excuse the injuries
That thou hast done me; therefore turn, and draw."
(Act 3 Scene 1)

TASK:

Do you agree that Tybalt's character "is very similar to how some young people act today"? Explain your answer.

What might a modern day Tybalt look and act like? Have you seen a character like this in a soap opera or a film?

PARIS

Although Paris is a minor character, he serves an important function: he unwittingly becomes a rival to Romeo, and his presence accelerates the play's events. The marriage is brought forward, meaning Juliet has to take the potion earlier; this in turn means Friar Laurence has less time to get the letter to Romeo, and so on.

When reading or watching the play, Paris's appearances (after his first one) often surprise people – we are so consumed by the relationship between Romeo and Juliet that it is easy to forget all about him until he actually re-appears!

Life treats Paris very unfairly in this play. He is a perfectly decent man – one who goes about everything in the "right" way, such as approaching Capulet to ask for Juliet's hand in marriage. He is grief-stricken by Juliet's "death," and when he goes to spend some quiet moments by her tomb, he fights Romeo to defend her honor, as he thinks Romeo is just out to cause anti-Capulet trouble.

Yet, when he is killed, most of us don't really experience any deep feeling of loss, even if it is touching that he asks to be laid with Juliet. We tend not to regret his death too much because Paris, rightly or wrongly, is seen as "getting in the way" of the romance we want to see – that of Romeo and Juliet.

Important quotations by Paris

"Younger than she are happy mothers made."
(Act 1 Scene 2)

"Happily met, my lady and my wife!"
(Act 4 Scene 1)

"Sweet flower, with flowers thy bridal bed I strew,"
(Act 5 Scene 3)

"Stop thy unhallow'd toil, vile Montague!
Can vengeance be pursu'd further than death?"
(Act 5 Scene 3)

"O, I am slain! If thou be merciful,
Open the tomb, lay me with Juliet."
(Act 5 Scene 3)

TASK:

Imagine you are Strasbourg, Paris's best friend, and he has asked you to be his best man at the wedding.

Read us your best man's speech!

BENVOLIO

Benvolio is one of those characters who are relentlessly "nice." There is no edge about him at all, which, in dramatic terms, is not always a good thing. We first meet him in the opening scene, when he is trying to stop people fighting. This is one of his main preoccupations throughout the play. He fails here, just as he fails again in Act 3 Scene 1.

He fails both times because of Tybalt; Tybalt and Benvolio are opposites in personality terms, one concerned with honor and violence, the other with peace and having a quiet life.

Of course, there's nothing at all wrong with being nice, and Benvolio proves himself a good friend to Romeo, being a shoulder to cry on when he's upset about Rosaline (Act 1 Scene 1) and persuading him to go to Capulet's party so that he can stop thinking about her (Act 1 Scene 2).

He is also a good-natured foil for some of Mercutio's barbed wit. In Act 3 Scene 1, Mercutio ridicules Benvolio's legendary mild temperament by creating a series of outlandish tales which are supposed to reflect what a hot-headed, fiery man Benvolio is!

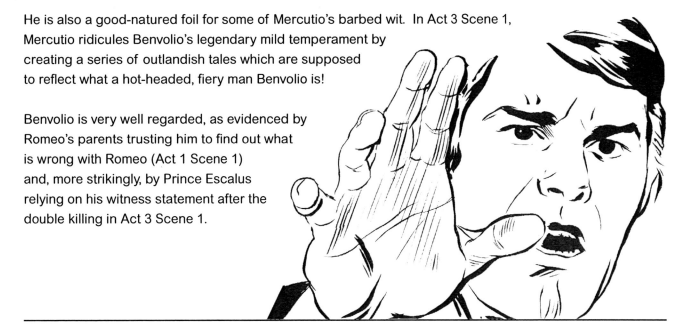

Benvolio is very well regarded, as evidenced by Romeo's parents trusting him to find out what is wrong with Romeo (Act 1 Scene 1) and, more strikingly, by Prince Escalus relying on his witness statement after the double killing in Act 3 Scene 1.

Important quotations by Benvolio

"I do but keep the peace: put up thy sword,
Or manage it to part these men with me."
(Act 1 Scene 1)

"I pray thee, good Mercutio, let's retire:
The day is hot, the Capulets abroad,
And, if we meet, we shall not 'scape a brawl;"
(Act 3 Scene 1)

"We talk here in the public haunt of men:
Either withdraw unto some private place,
Or reason coldly of your grievances,
Or else depart; here all eyes gaze on us."
(Act 3 Scene 1)

TASK:

Can someone be <u>too</u> nice? Explain your answer.

NURSE

The Nurse has a very special relationship with Juliet – much more special than a normal nurse or nanny. Indeed, she seems to have a much closer bond with Juliet than Lady Capulet does.

This is partly because the Nurse had a child, called Susan, at the same time Juliet was born. Susan died, and the Nurse seemed to direct her energies into baby Juliet, including breastfeeding her (we learn all this in Act 1 Scene 3).

The Nurse, unrequested, rattles off a host of fond and loving anecdotes about young Juliet. Lady Capulet never does. When Lord Capulet loses his temper over Juliet's refusal to marry Paris (Act 3 Scene 5), the Nurse defends her more forcefully than does Juliet's own mother. She does not share Mercutio's learning or linguistic skill, but she certainly shares both his fondness for talking and for lewdness!

At times – for both Romeo and the audience – the Nurse can be an incredibly annoying character. She always seems to be the one interrupting the lovers when they are together, and she takes what seems to be an incredibly long time (deliberately) to give Juliet her message from Romeo (Act 2 Scene 5).

The Nurse is a romantic herself and loves Juliet so much that she is prepared to go behind her parents' backs to help her marry Romeo. But, as romantic as she is, she is also very experienced and practical. The Nurse is only thinking of what's best for Juliet, and she doesn't realize how big a betrayal it is, when she advises Juliet to forget all about Romeo and marry Paris instead.

Important quotations by the Nurse

"Thou wast the prettiest babe that e'er I nurs'd:
An I might live to see thee married once,
I have my wish." (Act 1 Scene 3)

"Romeo's a dishclout to him:" (Act 3 Scene 5)

"Alas, alas! Help, help! my lady's dead!"
(Act 4 Scene 5)

TASK:

What do you think are the most important qualities a mother should have, and which of these does the Nurse display? Support your answer with reference to the text.

FRIAR LAURENCE

In many ways, Friar Laurence is to Romeo what the Nurse is to Juliet. Just as Juliet confides in the Nurse rather than her mother, Romeo goes straight to see Friar Laurence rather than his father.

The Friar is a strange contradiction. He is obviously an intelligent, educated man (he certainly impresses the Nurse in Act 3 Scene 3), but he makes some incredibly naive and plainly crazy decisions.

Did he really think that going behind the backs of both sets of parents by marrying their children would bring the families closer together? He is even more optimistic than that, saying it might turn their hatred into "pure love."

He gives out very wise and solid advice to Romeo, both before the events of the play begin (he has obviously counselled Romeo about Rosaline as we learn in Act 2 Scene 3) and during the play, especially when the fugitive Romeo hides out at his cell after killing Tybalt (Act 3 Scene 3).

Yet some of his own decisions are, to be polite, open to question. The situation Juliet presents him with in Act 4 Scene 1, i.e. that she has been ordered to marry Paris, is indeed very difficult…but his elaborate plan is fraught with risk. He might know his plants and herbs, but giving a young girl anything which mimics the signs of death for almost two whole days must carry huge danger. To top it all, at her moment of greatest need – when she wakes in the tomb and is greeted by the sight of her dead husband – he abandons her to save his own skin.

He confesses everything at the end of the play, and the Prince believes him, summing things up by saying, "We still have known thee for a holy man."

Important quotations by Friar Laurence

"Young men's love, then, lies
Not truly in their hearts, but in their eyes."
(Act 2 Scene 3)

"These violent delights have violent ends,
And in their triumph die: like fire and powder,
Which, as they kiss, consume."
(Act 2 Scene 6)

"For this alliance may so happy prove,
To turn your households' rancour to pure love."
(Act 2 Scene 3)

TASK:

Before he sends Friar John to Mantua with his letter, he decides to tell him all about the situation with Romeo and Juliet. Write a playscript of the conversation they have.

PRINCE ESCALUS

We only see the Prince *after* bad things have happened – and those things get increasingly more tragic. This indicates that although he has the authority in Verona, he is not fully in control.

He speaks powerfully but, as spelled out in the Prologue, it is only the deaths of Romeo and Juliet who can bring the feud to an end – the Prince, despite his efforts, was never going to achieve this.

He is by no means a weak character, and he makes good judgments at times. Although he previously said he would put to death anyone found guilty of shedding blood in Verona's streets, he realizes Romeo was provoked in the extreme by Tybalt and instead commits him to exile.

When he says in Act 5 Scene 3 that "All are punish'd" he means himself too. Not only have his citizens been affected, but he has lost two kinsmen in Mercutio and Paris. He blames himself for this, perhaps harshly, saying how he had been turning a blind eye to their behavior or, as he puts it, "winking at their discords."

Important quotations by Escalus

"If ever you disturb our streets again,
Your lives shall pay the forfeit of the peace."
(Act 1 Scene 1)

"And for that offence,
Immediately we do exile him hence:"
(Act 3 Scene 1)

"Where be these enemies? Capulet! Montague!
See, what a scourge is laid upon your hate,
That heaven finds means to kill your joys with
love!" (Act 5 Scene 3)

"And I, for winking at your discords too,
Have lost a brace of kinsmen: all are punish'd."
(Act 5 Scene 3)

"Go hence, to have more talk of these sad things;
Some shall be pardon'd, and some punished:
For never was a story of more woe,
Than this of Juliet and her Romeo."
(Act 5 Scene 3)

TASK:

Could the Prince have prevented the deaths in this play? How much is he to blame for what happened in Verona?

LORDS AND LADIES

Lord and Lady Montague are barely a presence in the play and are nowhere nearly as well defined as their Capulet equivalents.

Lord Capulet is seen as a warm and fun-loving man; even when he realizes Romeo has crashed his party, he speaks highly of the boy. But he also has a very fiery side, which is apparent when Tybalt challenges him and, more pointedly, when he loses his temper after Juliet refuses to marry Paris, hurling hurtful insults and threats at her as well as to her nurse. Despite that, he loves Juliet and is very upset by her death.

Lady Capulet appears as an aloof and cold woman early in the play, concerned more with her social status (i.e. encouraging Juliet to marry Paris) than she is with her daughter's happiness. When Juliet turns to her for help, she rejects her only daughter (Act 3 Scene 5). She suffers in direct comparison with the Nurse, but she does defend Juliet when Capulet attacks her, and she is grief-stricken by Juliet's "death" (Act 4 Scene 5). She obviously loved her daughter a great deal, but she seemed not to show that love until too late.

Important quotations by the Lords and Ladies

"What noise is this? Give me my long sword, ho!"
(Capulet, Act 1 Scene 1)

"Thou villain, Capulet! – Hold me not; let me go."
(Montague, Act 1 Scene 1)

"Am I the master here, or you? go to!"
(Capulet, Act 1 Scene 5)

"Prince, as thou art true,
For blood of ours, shed blood of Montague."
(Lady Capulet, Act 3 Scene 1)

"Romeo slew Tybalt, Romeo must not live."
(Lady Capulet, Act 3 Scene 1)

"Hang thee, young baggage! disobedient wretch!
I tell thee what: get thee to church
o' Thursday,
Or never after look me in the face."
(Capulet, Act 3 Scene 5)
"Talk not to me, for I'll not speak a word:
Do as thou wilt, for I have done with thee."
(Lady Capulet, Act 3 Scene 5)

"O brother Montague! give me thy hand:"
(Capulet, Act 5 Scene 3)

"For I will raise her statue in pure gold;"
(Montague, Act 5 Scene 3)

TASK:

How much are the parents to blame for the tragic end of *Romeo and Juliet?* Support your answer with reference to the text.

MATCHING QUOTATIONS

Cut out the all the cards and match the quotation to the character who said it!

Younger than she are happy mothers made.	**Nurse**
I pray thee, good Mercutio, let's retire: The day is hot, the Capulets abroad, And, if we meet, we shall not 'scape a brawl;	**Prince Escalus**
From ancient grudge break to new mutiny, Where civil blood makes civil hands unclean.	**Juliet**
Romeo slew Tybalt, Romeo must not live.	**Friar Laurence**
This, by his voice, should be a Montague. Fetch me my rapier, boy.	**Benvolio**
O calm, dishonourable, vile submission!	**Tybalt**

MATCHING QUOTATIONS

Cut out the all the cards and match the quotation to the character who said it!

There is no world without Verona walls;	**Mercutio**
Young men's love, then, lies Not truly in their hearts, but in their eyes.	**Capulet**
What's in a name? That which we call a rose, By any other word would smell as sweet;	**Romeo**
And I, for winking at your discords too, Have lost a brace of kinsmen; all are punish'd.	**Paris**
Alas, alas! Help, help! my lady's dead!	**Chorus (Prologue)**
Am I the master here, or you? go to!	**Lady Capulet**

CHARACTERS AND ADJECTIVES

If you are going to describe someone in detail, you need to use lots of adjectives.

TASK:

Below is a box that contains a wide variety of adjectives.

Which adjectives would you use to describe each character? You can use each adjective more than once, and you don't have to use them all.

headstrong	nasty
good-humored	loving
demanding	intimidating
charming	honorable
forgiving	cold
witty	threatening
kind	loyal
clever	foolish
helpful	naive
understanding	optimistic
weak	practical
temperamental	romantic
talkative	spirited
vicious	respectful
resilient	scary
strong	lively

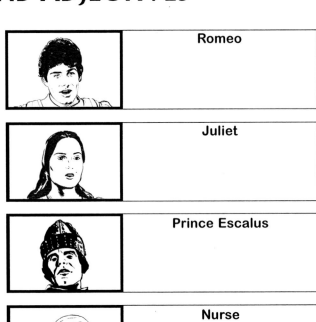

Romeo

Juliet

Prince Escalus

Nurse

Lord Capulet

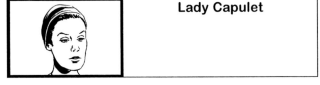

Lady Capulet

Mercutio

Tybalt

Friar Laurence

Benvolio

Paris

EXTENSION TASK:

Choose any character and support your choice of adjectives with excerpts from the play.
It doesn't necessarily have to be something the character says.

48

ADJECTIVES – WIDENING YOUR VOCABULARY

Adjectives are "describing words." If you want to describe something well, you need to use adjectives. Shakespeare used a wide variety of adjectives, many of which have fallen out of common usage now; however, others are still going strong.

The use of adjectives doesn't automatically stop writing from being boring. Too much use of the same adjectives, for instance, can quickly become tedious. Below is a list of commonly used adjectives. There is nothing wrong with these words, but some people use them all the time and don't bother thinking of alternatives that would improve their writing.

TASK:

Think of another word you could use for each of the common adjectives and add it under the "Your alternative" heading. Then use a thesaurus to find further alternatives. Widening your vocabulary (i.e. using a variety of different words) will almost certainly improve your writing…you might even become as good as Shakespeare!

Common adjective	Your alternative	Some from a thesaurus
good		
nice		
bad		
happy		
excited		
hungry		
slow		
quick		
wet		
hot		
dirty		
long		
old		

SIMILES

A "simile" is an expression in which you compare one thing to another using "as" or "like," e.g. "as quiet as a mouse" or "like a knife through butter."

A simile is an example of figurative language. Figurative language can be called "imagery," and the easiest way to think of this is something that puts a picture in your mind.

Adjectives are all well and good, but often a simile can be even more effective in getting a description across to a reader – especially if it is an unusual one that makes people think.

Shakespeare was very fond of them – did you notice any of these as you read the play?

On the left you will see a list of similes that appear in *Romeo and Juliet*. Can you come up with similes of your own?

Shakespeare's similes	Your similes
a bump as big as a young cockerel's stone	a bump as big as…
scaring the ladies like a crow-keeper	scaring the ladies like…
it pricks like thorn	it pricks like…
she hangs upon the cheek of night as a rich jewel in an Ethiop's ear	she hangs upon the cheek of night as…
the brightness of her cheek would shame those stars, as daylight doth a lamp	the brightness of her cheek would shame those stars, as…
love goes toward love, as schoolboys from their books	love goes toward love, as…
she looks as pale as any clout (dishrag) in the versal world (universe)	she looks as pale as…
as swift in motion as a ball	as swift in motion as…
unwieldy, slow, heavy and pale as lead	unwieldy, slow, heavy and pale as…
as gentle as a lamb	as gentle as…
in their triumph die: like fire and powder	in their triumph they die like…
thy head is as full of quarrels as an egg is full of meat	thy head is as full of quarrels as…
to't they go like lightning	to't they go like…
so tedious is this day, as is the night before some festival to an impatient child that hath new robes, and may not wear them	so tedious is this day as is…
pale as ashes	pale as…
like a misbehav'd and sullen wench, that pout'st upon thy fortune	like a… that pouts upon thy fortune
shrieks like mandrakes' torn out of the earth	shrieks like…
Death lies on her, like an untimely frost upon the sweetest flower of all the field	Death lies on her like…

METAPHORS

A "metaphor" is a type of comparison. It differs from a simile in that it does not say something is "like" or "as" something else, but borrows words and images to say one thing *is* another.

Metaphors, like similes, are examples of figurative language. Figurative language can be called "imagery," and the easiest way to think of this is something that puts a picture in your mind.

Whereas similes are sometimes more effective than simple adjectives when describing something, metaphors can be even better than similes.

Shakespeare used hundreds throughout his plays and poems – did you notice any as you read the play?

TASK:

On the left you will see a list of metaphors that appear in *Romeo and Juliet*. In the middle is a space for you to explain the metaphor in your own words. You don't necessarily have to relate your answer to the context of the play – just look at the words as they are. Two examples have been done for you. The third column gives space for you to write your own metaphors on the same theme.

Good luck – some of these are quite tricky!

Shakespeare's metaphors	What is he describing?	Your metaphors
heartless hinds	This is Tybalt comparing the weaker servants to female deer	
purple fountains issuing from your veins	blood pouring from wounds	
golden window of the east		
love is a smoke made with the fume of sighs		
I will make thee think they swan a crow		
He's a man of wax		

METAPHORS

Shakespeare's metaphors	What is he describing?	Your metaphors
I have a soul of lead		
dreams, which are the children of an idle brain		
a snowy dove trooping with crows		
my lips, two blushing pilgrims		
Juliet is the sun		
I have night's cloak to hide me		
I am fortune's fool		
Come, civil night, thou sober-suited matron, all in black		
Night's candles are burnt out, and jocund day stands tiptoe on the misty mountain tops		
you slug-a-bed!		
Thou detestable maw (stomach), thou womb of death, gorg'd with the dearest morsel of the earth		
winking at your discords		

OXYMORONS

Despite what you might think, an "oxymoron" is not a stupid person who survives on oxygen! It describes a technique in language when a writer or speaker juxtaposes (puts next to each other) two words which are usually opposite in meaning or sense. "Bitter sweet" is a well known one. "Oxymoron" comes from the Greek words *oxys* meaning "sharp" and *moros* meaning "dull."

Oxymorons can reflect a confused or upset state of mind. They can initially appear nonsensical; however, when you consider some of them, they can be very clever descriptions of the many things in life that aren't straightforward.

In *Romeo and Juliet*, almost all of them appear at or after moments of severe stress. Many are spoken by Romeo when sees the effects of the riot in Act 1 Scene 1 or by Juliet when she finds out that Romeo has killed Tybalt and been banished.

The oxymorons that appear in *Romeo and Juliet* are listed in the speech bubble below. The only problem is, the two halves of each oxymoron have been separated! Can you pair them up? Remember, you are trying to match opposites (not words which go together) so "angelical saint" is definitely NOT one, and neither is "damned villain"! Don't worry if you don't get them as they actually appear in the play: you never know, yours might be better than Shakespeare's!

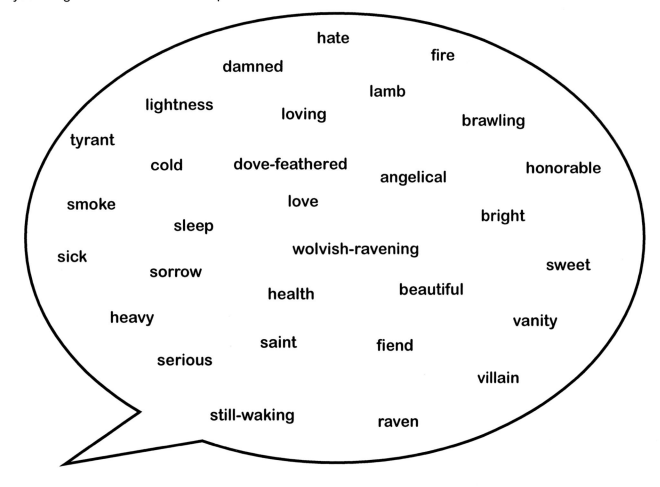

EXTENSION TASK:
Create some oxymorons of your own, using words other than those in the speech bubble above.

JULIET'S AMBIGUITY

Words and phrases are said to be "ambiguous" when they are open to interpretation or, put more simply, can have more than one meaning.

Part of Act 3 Scene 5 contains a large amount of ambiguity, displaying Shakespeare's wit and skill as a writer. Lady Capulet visits Juliet in her bedroom and finds her crying over Romeo's banishment but Lady Capulet assumes that she is crying over the death of Tybalt. Lady Capulet is, understandably, very critical of Romeo. Juliet loves him and refuses to criticize him but she also has to give replies to her mother that appear to do just the opposite so her mother doesn't suspect anything.

The scene is heavy with dramatic irony – we as an audience know much more than Lady Capulet, so we *should* be able to understand the double meaning, whereas she must take Juliet's words at face value.

In the following exercise, try to explain:
What Lady Capulet *thinks* Juliet means.
What Juliet *really* means.

The lines	What Lady Capulet *thinks* Juliet means	What Juliet *really* means
no man like he doth grieve my heart.		
Ay, madam, from the reach of these my hands: 'Would, none but I might venge my cousin's death!		
Indeed, I never shall be satisfied With Romeo, till I behold him – dead – Is my poor heart so for a kinsman vex'd.		
Madam, if you could find out but a man To bear a poison, I would temper it, That Romeo should, upon receipt thereof, Soon sleep in quiet. O! how my heart abhors		
To hear him nam'd, and cannot come to him, To wreak the love I bore my cousin Upon his body that hath slaughter'd him!		

MISSING WORDS

To complete the sentence below, underline the correct word in the box, then write it in the gap.

Be careful – there are a few traps!

1. Juliet is _____ years old in the play.

2. The town Romeo goes to when he is exiled
    is _____.

3. Mercutio is the Prince's _____.

4. _____ has a reputation of being a peace maker.

5. "That which we call a _____,
    By any other word would smell as sweet;"

6. Romeo and Juliet met on a _____ and were married
    on the _____.

7. "O, I am fortune's _____."

8. _____ dies of grief at the end of the play.

9. The person who informs Romeo of Juliet's death is
    _____.

10. "For never was a story of more _____,
    Than this of Juliet and her Romeo."

fool	Paris	cousin

Tuesday   flower

fifteen   woe   Monday

plaything   sadness

Wednesday   Verona

rose   Lady Montague

Friar Laurence   kinsman

fourteen   puppet

Benvolio   Lady Capulet

Balthasar

Prince Escalus   Mantua

tragedy   thirteen

Sunday

55

CLOSE TEXTUAL ANALYSIS

ACT 2 SCENE 2 – "THE BALCONY SCENE"

When reading a text, there are several degrees and levels of understanding. In fact, "getting it," or merely understanding, will only get you a passing grade. Familiarity will improve your grade, but you will need insight to push it higher.

Aim high! The best grades are usually given to writing that displays originality of analysis and interpretation. That might sound difficult (OK, it is difficult!) but it isn't as hard as it sounds. It means, in simple terms, that you should try to read between the lines: look at the words for more than the obvious meanings and try to come up with some of your own ideas about the language, characters, themes or whatever it is you want to mention!

If you want to do well in English, English Literature or a whole host of other subjects, you need to look at the text very closely and develop your skills of textual analysis.

The following exercise gives you some lines from Act 2 Scene 2 that are worth looking at more closely. It helps if you know the scene well, but you can still take a shot, even if you are unfamiliar with the scene.

TASK:

Study the following lines and write about what you think they mean. Some might be simple and require only basic answers; others have lots of potential for you to show off your analysis and interpretation! If you are stuck from the outset, your teacher will be able to help you and maybe provide you with one or two examples.

CLOSE TEXTUAL ANALYSIS

ACT 2 SCENE 2 – "THE BALCONY SCENE"

1. He jests at scars that never felt a wound.

2. But, soft! what light through yonder window breaks?
    It is the east, and Juliet is the sun!

3. The brightness of her cheek would shame those stars,
    As daylight doth a lamp; her eyes in heaven,
    Would through the airy region stream so bright,
    That birds would sing and think it were not night.

4. O Romeo, Romeo! wherefore art thou Romeo?
    Deny thy father, and refuse thy name;
    Or, if thou wilt not, be but sworn my love,
    And I'll no longer be a Capulet.

5. What's in a name? That which we call a rose,
    By any other word would smell as sweet;

6. My ears have yet not drunk a hundred words
    Of thy tongue's uttering, yet I know the sound.

7. (Juliet) If they do see thee, they will murder thee.
    (Romeo) Alack! there lies more peril in thine eye
    Than twenty of their swords: look thou but sweet,
    And I am proof against their enmity.

8. O gentle Romeo!
    If thou dost love, pronounce it faithfully;
    Or if thou think'st I am too quickly won,
    I'll frown, and be perverse, and say thee nay,
    So thou wilt woo; but, else, not for the world.

9. Do not swear at all;
    Or, if thou wilt, swear by thy gracious self,
    Which is the god of my idolatry,
    And I'll believe thee.

10. O blessed, blessed night! I am afeard,
    Being in night, all this is but a dream,
    Too flattering-sweet to be substantial.

FORMAL DEBATE

A formal debate is where a "motion" (a suggestion, idea, or statement) is "proposed" for discussion. There are two teams, and each team must convince the rest of the group to vote for them, thereby winning the debate. Everyone involved in the debate comes under the title of the "house."

One person will act as "Chair" and control the debate. Everyone must respect the Chair or things will quickly fall apart!

The two teams are each made up of two speakers. The speakers – unless they are very talented indeed! – will need to have been given some time in which to prepare their speeches.

For the motion   **Against the motion**

Proposer _____   **Opposer** _____

Seconder _____   **Seconder** _____

The rest of the group, or class, make up the "floor" and will be able to ask questions at the appropriate time.

1.   The Chair says, "The motion upon which this house will debate is '(title of motion – see below for suggestions)'. I now call upon (name of Proposer) to propose the motion."

2.   The Proposer gives a short, prepared, and hopefully convincing speech to the rest of the House in favor of the motion. The Chair decides how long this should last, but five minutes is a good maximum. Every speech by the four speakers begins, "Chair, ladies and gentlemen…"

3.   The Chair says, "I now call upon (name of Opposer) to oppose the motion."

4.   The Opposer gives his or her speech, which will disagree with the motion.

5.   The Chair then introduces the Seconder for the motion. The Seconder's job is to support what the Proposer has said, perhaps introducing new points and, if possible, responding to what the Opposer has just said!

6.   The Chair then introduces the Seconder against the motion.

7.   When all four speeches are finished, the Chair says, "I will now open the debate to questions from the floor."

8.   Anyone who is not the Chair or a team member can ask a question or make a point – but make sure you name the team member to whom you're talking to at the very beginning; otherwise it can get very confusing.

9.   People from the floor should not just make general points – each must get a response from one of the four team members!

FORMAL DEBATE

10.   The Chair will decide when time is up. He or she will then say, "I am now closing the debate. I would like to ask (name of one of the team members speaking for the motion) to sum up." This is the last chance for the team members to try to convince the floor to vote for them. Again, it is up to the Chair how long to give each speaker for "summing up."

11.   The Chair will then say, "I would like to ask (name of one of the team members speaking against the motion) to sum up."

12.   When the team speaking against the motion has finished summing up, the Chair will say, "The house will now vote upon the motion: (title of motion). Can I see votes for the motion? (The Chair will then count the votes which are cast by the floor, raising a hand if they wish to vote in favor of the motion). Can I see votes against the motion? (Again, the Chair counts)."

13.   If it is a tie, the Chair has the casting vote. The Chair then says, "I declare that the motion is carried/rejected by x votes to y. Thank you all for taking part in today's debate."

Some suggestions for formal debate, related to *Romeo and Juliet*:

- "Love at first sight doesn't really exist"

- "Parents put too much pressure on their children"

- "Children need very strong guidance and direction because they have no experience"

- "The legal age for everything – including marriage – should be raised to 21"

Some classic motions:

- "This school should adopt/abandon school uniforms"

- "Students get too much homework"

- "Prison life is too easy for convicted criminals"

- "Sports and film stars earn too much money"

- "Television is harmful, and children watch too much of it"

PLAYSCRIPT WRITING AND PERFORMANCE – "THE SCENE UNSEEN"

TASK:

On the next page is a set of cards that outline different scenarios based on events in *Romeo and Juliet*.

The thing is, they don't appear in the play!

You (and the rest of your group, depending on which card you choose or are given) will have to write a playscript for the scenario stated on the card. Then, depending on your teacher, you might very well have to read out (or even act out!) your playscript. You do not have to write it in Shakespearean language – though you might want to try to incorporate a flavor of old language.

GUIDANCE

If possible, have a look at a playscript to remind yourself how they are set out on the page.

It will look something like this:

> It is outside the Capulet mansion, and the party is still in full swing. Tybalt has just stormed out, angry and embarrassed, after being put in his place by Capulet. Tybalt wanted to attack Romeo, who had crashed the party. Sampson and Gregory are outside the mansion having a chat. Unable to contain his anger, Tybalt speaks to the pair.
>
> Tybalt: For shame! A Montague should NEVER be allowed into Capulet grounds!
> Sampson: I beg your pardon, sir? A Montague at the party?
> Tybalt: Yes, that damned villain Romeo!

- Start with a brief introduction to put your scene into context.

- Every time characters speak, write their names on the left of the page and follow each one with a colon (:).

- You will not write much description. It should be mainly "dialogue" (what the characters say). If you need to give the actors any hints on how lines should be said, do it briefly and put it in parentheses.

- Make sure you write for your characters as they are in the story. In other words, make sure each speaker "stays in character." As you can see in the example above. Tybalt is fiery and angry; Sampson is courteous and calm (at the moment, that is!)

- The cards state a minimum number of characters for each scenario. It is given as a minimum because you or your teacher might want you to introduce other characters into the scene.

- The scenarios are only a starting point – develop them as you wish (within reason)!

- If you are asked to read or act out your playscript, make sure you practice it first – as a group.

THE SCENARIOS

Scenario 1

Parts: 2 minimum

In Act 1 Scene 1, **Lord Montague** said how he and his friends had tried in vain to find out what was wrong with **Romeo**.

He tries again. This is before Romeo meets Juliet. Perhaps he will be more talkative this time…or perhaps not!

(Other suggested parts – Lady Montague, Benvolio, Mercutio)

Scenario 2

Parts: 3 minimum

Tybalt has just left the Capulet ball after being told off by Capulet. Outside the house, enraged, he talks with Capulet servants **Sampson** and **Gregory** about what he is going to do next regarding Romeo, who crashed the party.

(Other suggested parts – Paris, Lady Capulet, Peter, create some other Capulets)

Scenario 3

Parts: 2 minimum

Paris meets **Juliet** at the Capulet party before she has met Romeo. He tries to tell her how much he likes her and that he would like to marry her. How would Juliet react?

(Other suggested parts – Romeo! The Nurse, Capulet, Lady Capulet)

Scenario 4

Parts: 2 minimum

It is immediately after the deaths of Mercutio and Tybalt, and Romeo has been exiled. Things are getting out of control in Verona. **Prince Escalus** discusses with **an adviser** how best to restore peace.

(Other suggested parts – more advisers, Capulet, Montague)

Scenario 5

Parts: 2 minimum

Friar Laurence is about to give his letter for Romeo to **Friar John**. At his wit's end with worry, he confesses to John what he has done. Friar John offers his advice.

(Other suggested parts – another Friar, Benvolio)

Scenario 6

Parts: 2 minimum

It is after the funerals of Romeo and Juliet. **Capulet** and **Montague** discuss the past, present and future.

(Other suggested parts – Lady Capulet, Benvolio)

CASTING DIRECTOR'S PLANNING NOTES

TASK:

You are a casting director for a stage production of *Romeo and Juliet*. Below is the sheet of paper on which you are making some notes on what you are looking for in the actors.

What emotions will actors need to work on to give a good performance in each role? What do you think they should look like? How old do you think they should be?

What type of clothes will you need to ask the wardrobe department to find? (N.B. This is very much affected by the period in which you want to set your production. In 1600? World War Two? Now? You might very well have to do some research in this area.)

You can do this activity on your own or in a small team. The director has the final say, but it is always good to get input from other people – and this is what would happen in any good production!

ROMEO
Emotions:

Physical appearance:

Age:
Clothes:

JULIET
Emotions:

Physical appearance:

Age:
Clothes:

MERCUTIO
Emotions:

Physical appearance:

Age:
Clothes:

TYBALT
Emotions:

Physical appearance:

Age:
Clothes:

NURSE
Emotions:

Physical appearance:

Age:
Clothes:

CASTING DIRECTOR'S PLANNING NOTES

FRIAR LAURENCE
Emotions:

Physical appearance:

Age:
Clothes:

LORD CAPULET
Emotions:

Physical appearance:

Age:
Clothes:

LADY CAPULET
Emotions:

Physical appearance:

Age:
Clothes:

BENVOLIO
Emotions:

Physical appearance:

Age:
Clothes:

PARIS
Emotions:

Physical appearance:

Age:
Clothes:

PRINCE ESCALUS
Emotions:

Physical appearance:

Age:
Clothes:

Other characters you might wish to consider are minor ones:
**Montague, Lady Montague, Chorus, Abraham, Balthasar,
Sampson, Gregory, Peter, Friar John, Apothecary,
Cousin Capulet, Musicians, Watchmen, Citizens, masquers**

AFTER THE DEATHS – THE INQUEST

A HOTSEATING EXERCISE

Events in Verona have sent shock waves throughout Italy. King Rudolf II has sent a small team of trusted advisers to investigate events.

The team consists of:

- Bishop Roderigo (a devout holy man)
- Prince Valentine (equal to Prince Escalus in status but from a different region)
- Count Ludovico (a legal expert used to questioning people)

They will (either individually or as a group, as decided by your teacher) interview the following witnesses (not necessarily in this order):

| Prince Escalus | Capulet | Lady Capulet | Montague | Benvolio | Nurse | Friar Laurence |

The team of investigators will not know as much about the events as you do. They first need to find out the basics of who the witnesses actually are and what happened and why before asking more probing questions about actions, blame, etc.

Bear in mind that because you have seen the entire play, you know more than all of the characters (and the investigators). You have seen everything – they have only witnessed a selection.

Good luck…especially if you are being questioned!

The team of investigators can come up with a judgment after everyone has been interviewed. They have the power to apportion blame and to sentence individuals, if necessary!

JULIET'S "SUICIDE" NOTE

In Act 4 Scene 3, Juliet drinks the potion given to her by Friar Laurence. Before she takes it, she speaks about the many things which concern her. One of her worries is that the potion will not merely make her unconscious, but will actually kill her. This is completely understandable: any potion that can mimic the signs of death and will knock her out for almost two days must be very strong – and she is only a young girl, after all. Such is the strength of her feelings for Romeo that she is prepared to take the risk – but she isn't very confident. Just in case things go wrong and she doesn't survive, imagine that she writes a note, which she seals in an envelope and addresses, ensuring it will be read by that person. It is up to you to decide who the note is addressed to. Romeo? The Nurse? Her mother and father? You may decide that she needs to write more than one note.

TASK:
Write Juliet's "suicide note."

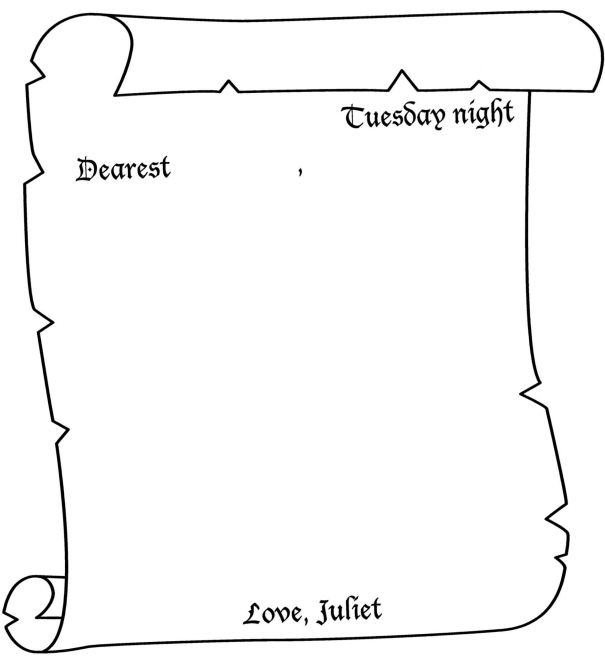

CHARACTER DIARIES

Keeping a diary or journal is a very traditional and popular way of bringing together one's thoughts. It also serves as something the writer can look back on at a later date. Some people write diaries because it helps them think or provides "catharsis" – a release of strong emotions.

Choose one of the characters below, then choose one the parts of the play listed. Write the character's diary entry for that time. The style of your writing might very well be affected by the character you choose and his or her personality.

Benvolio

1. After Act 1 Scene 1. He has been present at a riot, attacked by Tybalt, and had a conversation with Romeo about Rosaline.

2. After the killings of Mercutio and Tybalt. Romeo has been banished, and Benvolio has to explain everything to the Prince. Remember though, even Benvolio knows nothing about Juliet at this point.

3. After the events of the play are concluded. He has found out about Juliet but has lost his friend Romeo.

Romeo

1. Just before the start of the play when he is lovesick about Rosaline.

2. After the Balcony Scene. (Act 2 Scene 2)

3. In Mantua, waiting for news from Friar Laurence, before Balthasar arrives.

Juliet

1. After Act 1 Scene 3. She has been told about Paris's proposal. It is before the party.

2. After the Balcony Scene. (Act 2 Scene 2)

3. Trapped in her bedroom after being ordered to marry Paris. It is before she goes to see Friar Laurence.

THE VERONA NEWS

The events in many stories would never make the news, but imagine the talk in Verona about the things that happen in *Romeo and Juliet*. Such extreme events would be big news! After all, there is rioting, murder, a secret marriage, and the double suicide of two young people from the two most prominent families of the city. Just in case the audience misses the general significance of the events to Verona citizens, Shakespeare makes it very clear at both the beginning and the end of the play.

Citizens and officers in Act 1 Scene 1 shout, "Down with the Capulets! Down with the Montagues!" and Prince Escalus says the families "have thrice disturb'd the quiet of our streets,/And made Verona's ancient citizens/Cast by their grave beseeming ornaments,/To wield old partisans." In the last scene of the play, Lady Capulet says, "O, the people in the street cry, 'Romeo,'/Some 'Juliet,' and some 'Paris,' and all run/With open outcry toward our monument."

Verona citizens – and perhaps even people outside the city – would definitely like to know more about these events. It's front page news!

TASK:

Choose a key moment in the play and write a front page news story about it.

Remember to get the "five W's" into your piece as soon as possible: **What? Who? Where? When? Why?** The job of a news journalist is to give as much information as succinctly as possible and then progressively to give more details.

Try to incorporate some of the language of the play. Get "quotations" from key witnesses – these can either be lifted from the play, if appropriate, or created by you based on what you know about the characters.

You could write in the style of an "in your face" tabloid or a more reserved broadsheet (ask your teacher for examples) or simply write a straight story.

The example on the next page is based on the events of Act 1 Scene 1.

THE VERONA NEWS

Act 1 Scene 1 is a good choice, as are Act 3 Scene 1 (deaths of Mercutio and Tybalt) and Act 5 Scene 3 (the end of the play).

The Verona News
LATE MORNING EDITION

Prince threatens rioters with death
Capulets and Montagues at it again
By Giorgio Barmyarmy

An enraged Prince Escalus issued an ultimatum to the heads of the warring Capulet and Montague families after more public rioting yesterday afternoon.

For the third time in recent weeks, members of the rival families brawled publicly, this time on Via Rosa, and had to be separated by Officers of the Watch and several of Verona's more aged citizens.

Prince Escalus has made numerous requests for the fighting to cease and has now vowed to issue the death sentence to anyone who goes against that request.

"If ever you disturb our streets again," said the moved Prince, "your lives shall pay the forfeit of the peace."

EXTENSION TASK:

Try writing a more biased piece, favoring one of the families. Write a showbiz/gossip column for a magazine based on the Capulets' party. If you kept your eyes open, there was a lot to write about!

FILM REVIEW

A film review is an opinion piece, designed to inform and persuade the reader to go see the movie (or to avoid it, if it is poor!). Unless the film is a work of genius or is absolutely dire, most reviews contain both positive and negative elements. This requires a particular skill, as a reviewer needs to be able to make detailed comments without giving away key parts of the plot, which might spoil the film for those who want to see it. Fortunately, this isn't a major consideration for *Romeo and Juliet* as there are very few people who don't already know at least the outline of the plot.

Things a reviewer might consider are:

- Performances of the actors
- The director's interpretation of events
- The setting
- The costumes/clothing
- The length of the film

The important thing to develop in your writing (and your speaking as well) is an ability to justify or explain your views.

There is little point in simply writing, "Claire Danes is great, and so is Leonardo di Caprio." You might very well be right...but you need to focus on what it is about their performances that makes you think that way.

Feel free to comment on particular scenes and say why you like or dislike them.

If you know the playscript well, you might want to comment on things that are markedly different from Shakespeare's version. For example, in Zeffirelli's version, Paris is removed from the last scene – do you think this was a good or bad decision?

There are two particularly popular film versions of *Romeo and Juliet*:

- *Romeo and Juliet* (directed by Franco Zeffirelli, 1968)
- *William Shakespeare's Romeo + Juliet* (directed by Baz Luhrmann, 1996)

Write your own film review of a version of *Romeo and Juliet*. It may be one of the above two films or another production. It may even be a drama review if you have seen the play performed in a theater.

EXTENSION TASK:

If you want to do a more comprehensive and analytical piece of work, you could always compare two or more versions. To compare them in their entirety is rather ambitious. An excellent choice (because they are usually so different) is to compare the different interpretations of Act 3 Scene 1.

VERONA OBITUARIES

An obituary is a report, usually appearing in a newspaper, that gives the news of someone's death and records brief details about the person's life.

Here is the beginning of an entirely fictitious obituary, just as an example:

> "Ed Johnson, winner of four Olympic gold medals, died on Monday at the age of 80.
> Mr. Johnson passed away peacefully in his sleep at home in Naperville, IL. He leaves a wife, Annie, three children and four grandchildren.
> Ed, or "Jet Johnson" as he was known in the athletics world, enjoyed great success in the national college championships and led the American sprint team in the 1952 and 1956 Olympics.
> A notorious practical joker, Johnson was a popular character off-field and was much loved by the fans too.
> His greatest achievement was winning three gold medals at the 1952 Olympics in Helsinki, Finland, setting a world record in the 200 meters.
> He retired from professional athletics in 1958 and continued to coach young athletes until the 1980s."

TASK:

On the opposite page is a sheet for you to write an obituary for a character of your choice, which is to appear in his or her local newspaper.

As this is a tragedy, you have plenty to choose from:

- Romeo
- Juliet
- Mercutio
- Tybalt
- Paris
- Lady Montague

Whichever you choose, you can use the playscript to help you with some of the details of your character's life, but feel free to make up other things.

Write in the third person (your teacher will help you with this) and imagine the reader doesn't know your chosen character.

Underneath the word "Obituary," write the name of your chosen character.

OBITUARY

_____

(born   , died   )

by _____

MAGAZINE INTERVIEW WITH A CHARACTER OF YOUR CHOICE

Lots of magazines have interviews with famous people – it is often interesting to read about the lives of those in the public eye. There are several different types of interview, but the easiest to both read and write are "Question and Answer" (Q and A).

As you might guess, this type of interview simply states the question and then gives the interviewee's answer.

TASK:

Write a Q and A interview with one of the following – Lord Capulet, Lord Montague or Prince Escalus. Imagine that it is a couple of years after the end of *Romeo and Juliet*.

If you wish, you can use the example below (which chooses Lord Capulet) as a beginning, or you can start your own from scratch. Don't forget to ask your interviewee about past events and his or her attitude and behavior when Romeo and Juliet were still alive.

Verona Today LATE MORNING EDITION

Interview with Lord Capulet

In this issue of *Verona Today* we interview prominent citizen and head of one of the city's most famous families, Lord Capulet.

Q: Lord Capulet, I know you might find it difficult to talk about this, but I want to ask you about the days of your feud with the Montague family.

A: That's fine, I understand people want to know about it. I regret it deeply and the effect it had on both our families – and also the fine citizens of Verona.

Q: How exactly did the feud begin?

A: It all goes back to when my grandfather and the grandfather of Lord Montague argued over a business deal…

A MODERN VERSION OF *ROMEO AND JULIET*

TASK:

Write a twenty-first century short story or play based on Shakespeare's late sixteenth-century play.

You do not have to include every single element. In fact, it would be very ambitious to try to do so!

Some questions to consider and perhaps discuss with a partner or your class:

• Where will your story or play be set?

• Will the rivalry be over family or something else? (Neighborhood? Race? Music? Religion? Sport? Business?)

• How will Romeo and Juliet meet?

• What weapons, if any, will be used?

• What type of jobs will the likes of Nurse and Friar Laurence have?

• What position of authority will the equivalent of the Prince hold? (In Luhrmann's 1996 film version, they made him a police captain).

• Will you keep the same tragic ending? (it's your story, so you could change it!)

(N.B. Write a bullet point plan for your story or play first. You might realize that it will be very long, so you can reduce it at this point rather than becoming disheartened when you are halfway through!)

ESSAY WRITING

GCSE English and English Literature essay

Title:

"Here's much to do with hate, but more with love." Compare the presentation of hate and love in *Romeo and Juliet*, with specific reference to Act 1 Scene 1 and Act 2 Scene 2. Is the play more about love or hate?

Information:

To qualify for the highest grades, you must consider:

- the moral, philosophical and social significance of the text
- the writer's narrative craft and appeal to the reader
- details of language exploited for implication or suggestion
- social and historical context
- literary tradition

This sounds very complicated and challenging, but don't worry! Your teacher will help you, and also you can follow the plan below:

Plan:

1. Introduce the play by saying it is full of both love and hate. These were (and still are!) very popular and traditional themes to write about. Do some research (or see "*Romeo and Juliet* – Shakespeare's story?" from the Background section of this book!) and write a paragraph on how the story has been handed down over the years.

2. Discuss the hatred displayed in Act 1 Scene 1. Right from the earliest lines, the servants go out of their way to engage in conflict, Tybalt inflames it, and the Prince reveals that this is the third time the families have brawled in the streets. The citizens are also tired of the fighting. Perhaps discuss the concept of "honor" and how it was displayed in late 16c. Italy (is it much different from today?)

3. Discuss how the mood of the play changes when Romeo enters Act 1 Scene 1. He is lovesick. Look specifically at his use of oxymorons to show how confusing love and hate can be for people (Romeo in this case).

4. Move on to look at Act 2 Scene 2 in detail, explaining how Shakespeare makes it such a romantic scene.

5. Answer the question, "Is the play more about love or hate?" ensuring you support your opinions with references to the play.

Resist the temptation to re-tell chunks of the story. If you write what happens in the play, it should be because you are going to make a point about it!

Remember: **P**oint
                   Evidence
                   Explanation

In your "explanation" sections, ensure from time to time you comment on the *language* used in your "evidence" and how it "works." Comment on Shakespeare's skill/craft as a writer.

ESSAY WRITING

"Point, Evidence, Explanation" – example

When you are writing an essay, especially one which is based on a text, the "Point, Evidence, Explanation" model of writing is a simple and effective way of making sure you are keeping on track.

Point – the idea you want to put across, the point you are making – this is done briefly.

Evidence – this is where you back your point up by using a quotation or reference to something in the text.

Explanation – this is where you fully explain your point, usually referring to the evidence.

Everyone might have similar or even the same points and evidence. The real difference comes in the "explanation" section – this is your main opportunity to show how well you have understood the text (and the question) and to show off your writing skills.

Say that I am tackling point 2 of the essay plan, how Shakespeare creates an atmosphere of hatred in Act 1 Scene 1. There are many points that I could make. Here is an example:

Point – Right from the opening of the play, Shakespeare wants to make it clear that, for the Capulets and Montagues anyway, Verona is a world of constant violence and upheaval.

Evidence – Sampson: I strike quickly, being moved…A dog of the house of Montague moves me.

Explanation – These are lines **five** and **seven** of the play. Shakespeare immediately sets a provocative tone of menace for both the audience and the characters on stage. The choice of "dog" is deliberate – so deep is their animosity that even an animal of the rival house will "move" Sampson. It could also be a metaphor, indicating Sampson's hatred of the Montagues, referring to each member of their family as a dog! He needs little excuse to break out into violence. In fact, as we soon witness, they deliberately go looking for opportunities to create disorder.

This is work at the highest level. Go for it! You might not write as much as this, but the principle is always the same – Point, Evidence, Explanation.

(Top tip – don't forget to vary your sentences and vocabulary, especially the sentences which begin your paragraphs. If you write every Point, Evidence and Explanation in the same way, your essay will become boring very quickly! Your teacher will help you with this.)

ROMEO AND JULIET SPELLING JUMBLE

The words below are all either names of characters or words associated with the play. Unscramble the letters and write the correct spelling.

Jumbled Spelling	Correct Spelling
NICE PR	
ORE VAN	
MORGUE NAME TOO	
PLACATE DULY	
A FUNERAL CRIER	
A TROPHY ACE	
OUT CRIME	
AUNT MA	
POOR GLUE	
ENSCONCE ABLY	
LETTUCE JAIL UP	
HARDLINE'US PAL	

ROMEO AND JULIET WORD SEARCH

The following words are hidden in the grid below. Can you find them?

ROMEO	JULIET	VERONA	PRINCE
POISON	BENVOLIO	CAPULET	MONTAGUE
MERCUTIO	TYBALT	NURSE	POTION
FRIAR	LAURENCE	DAGGER	ROSE
BALCONY	PARIS	EXILE	MANTUA

```
B  A  L  C  O  N  Y  A  D  A  G  G  E  R  P
A  J  U  L  W  M  U  N  B  R  P  S  X  R  A
L  U  V  S  O  T  C  I  V  E  F  R  I  A  R
A  L  P  T  N  U  S  P  Y  W  E  I  L  O  U
M  I  E  A  U  R  O  I  T  U  C  R  E  M  T
N  E  M  R  I  A  C  I  B  D  L  K  N  E  O
I  T  L  A  B  Y  T  I  L  P  A  R  I  S  Y
M  O  O  N  S  R  O  M  E  O  N  U  R  S  E
O  M  K  O  S  U  M  C  X  T  V  T  E  R  C
N  W  L  R  M  B  N  C  L  I  O  N  E  L  N
T  A  D  E  U  I  A  S  C  O  H  G  E  H  E
A  Z  E  V  R  G  M  B  E  N  A  C  I  B  R
G  Q  S  P  O  I  S  O  N  S  S  R  P  B  U
U  B  O  T  C  A  P  U  L  E  T  R  O  S  A
E  C  R  X  E  M  N  L  A  S  C  B  T  I  L
```

ROMEO AND JULIET CROSSWORD

Try to complete this without using a copy of the play or any book to help you!

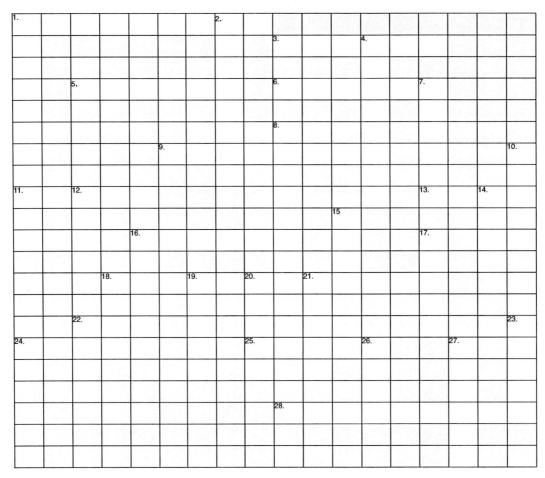

Romeo and Juliet crossword – The Clues

Across

1   The town where the playwright ("The Bard") was born (9)
3   The town Romeo goes to after his banishment (6)
5   "There is no world without _____ walls" (6)
6   The only girl to speak in the play (6)
9   Romeo's surname (8)
11 Lord Capulet is this, when Juliet tells him that she won't marry Paris (5)
13 Juliet is laid in the Capulet ____ (4)
16 This man says how "all are punish'd"(6)
18 What Juliet uses to finally kill herself (6)
21 The name of Nurse's servant (5)
24 The famous theater, associated with "The Bard" (5)

25 Prince: "And for that offence/Immediately we do _____ him hence" (5)
28 This man breaks the news of Juliet's death to Romeo (9)

Down

1   The surname of the playwright often called "The Bard" (11)
2   The name of Romeo's ex-girlfriend (8)
4   Juliet's age (8)
7   The Prince of Cats (6)
8   Juliet's surname (7)
10 The fairies' midwife is Queen ___ (3)
12 The material from which statues will be made at the end of the story (4)
14 Romeo offers to swear his love by this, but Juliet says it is inconstant (4)

15 On his wedding night, Romeo uses a ladder made of this to climb up to Juliet's bedroom (4)
16 Mercutio curses both families with his last words: "A _____ o' both your houses!" (6)
17 The name of the person who raised Juliet (5)
19 Juliet thinks she sees the _____ of Tybalt on her balcony before she takes the potion (5)
20 The Montagues' only child (5)
21 The man who asks Lord Capulet for his daughter's hand in marriage (5)
22 "A ____ by any other word would smell as sweet" (4)
23 Laurence and John are both one of these (5)
26 "It is the ____ and Juliet is the sun" (4)
27 The apothecary sells this to Romeo (6)

78

EDUCATIONAL WEBSITE LINKS

PROMOTING LITERACY IN THE CLASSROOM:-

Graphic Novels for Multiple Literacies
www.readingonline.org/newliteracies/jaal/11-02_column/
Gretchen E. Schwarz

The Graphic Classroom
http://graphicclassroom.blogspot.com/

Graphic novels - engaging readers and encouraging literacy
www.ltscotland.org.uk/literacy/findresources/graphicnovels/index.asp   **Learning and Teaching Scotland**

Comics Scholarship
www.dr-mel-comics.co.uk/sources/academic.html
Mel Gibson

Expanding Literacies through Graphic Novels
www.readwritethink.org/lessons/lesson_view.asp?id=1102
Gretchen E. Schwarz

Eek! Comics in the Classroom!
www.education-world.com/a_curr/profdev/profdev105.shtml
Education World

Comics in Education
www.humblecomics.com/comicsedu/   **Gene Yang**

Graphic Novels and Curriculum Integration
http://members.shaw.ca/yaying/518final/integ.html
ESL Teaching in Canada

The Secret Origin of Good Readers
www.night-flight.com/secretorigin/index.html

MAKING COMICS AND GRAPHIC NOVELS:-

National Association of Comic Art Educators
www.teachingcomics.org   **NACAE**

Scrap Comics
http://escrapbooking.com/projects/scrapcomic/index.htm
Eduscapes

Comic Life
http://plasq.com/comiclife

SHAKESPEARE GENERAL INTEREST:-

Shakespeare Magazine
http://shakespearemag.com/intro.asp

Shaksper - the Global Electronic Shakespeare Conference
www.shaksper.net/

Shakespeare Birthplace Trust
www.shakespeare.org.uk

Mr William Shakespeare and the Internet
http://shakespeare.palomar.edu

Shakespeare Resource Center
www.bardweb.net

The Shakespeare Mystery
www.pbs.org/wgbh/pages/frontline/shakespeare/

TO BE, OR NOT TO BE – THAT IS THE QUESTION
TEACHERS' VERSION
ANSWERS: (PAGE 8 & 9)

	True or False?
1. Shakespeare was born in Stratford-upon-Avon in 1564	True
2. His life and times are well documented	False
3. Shakespeare's family were very poor	False
4. He never went to school	False
5. William Shakespeare married Anne Hathaway	True
6. The whole Shakespeare family moved to London in 1587	False
7. Shakespeare's group of actors performed his plays for King James I	True
8. Shakespeare died in London	False
9. Shakespeare was buried in Stratford-upon-Avon in 1616	True
10. Descendants of Shakespeare are still alive today	False

FAMOUS SHAKESPEARE QUOTATIONS
TEACHERS' VERSION
ANSWER: (PAGE 11)

WISE WORDS	YOUR INTERPRETATION:
"Out, out, brief candle! Life's but a walking shadow, a poor player, That struts and frets his hour upon the stage, And then is heard no more. It is a tale Told by an idiot, full of sound and fury, Signifying nothing." *Macbeth*	Macbeth has just found out his wife has killed herself, and it makes him think of how pointless and worthless life is. He says living is rather like being a poor actor in a very bad play. It has been told by an "idiot," meaning that life is rather stupid and amounts to absolutely nothing in the long run – "signifying nothing."
"As flies to wanton boys are we to th' gods, They kill us for their sport." *King Lear*	These desperate and pessimistic words are spoken by the troubled Gloucester. Things have gone so badly for him he feels as if a vicious God were deliberately torturing him for his own satisfaction – rather like a cruel boy picking the wings off an innocent fly for his own enjoyment.
"Excellent wretch! Perdition catch my soul But I do love thee! and when I love thee not, Chaos is come again." *Othello*	Othello is deeply in love with his recently married wife, Desdemona. "Wretch" is normally used insultingly, but here he is being playful. Such is the depth of emotion he feels, he notes (with deep foreshadowing of later tragic events) that if he ever falls out of love with her, the world will fall into chaos for all concerned.
"Neither a borrower nor a lender be, For loan oft loses both itself and friend, And borrowing dulls the edge of husbandry." *Hamlet*	Polonius gives this oft-quoted advice to his son, Laertes. If you lend money to someone, there is a chance you may never get it back. If this happens, you lose both the money and the friendship. If you borrow money yourself, you might become reliant on this and lose all your skills of "making do."
"Uneasy lies the head that wears a crown." *Henry IV, Part II*	Many of Shakespeare's characters are troubled royals. Here, King Henry sums up the situation for everyone. He might be powerful and have the crown, but the head upon which it sits can never really rest due to the enormous weight of responsibility the king carries and the constant troubles, such as conspiracy, that come with being King.
"All the world's a stage, And all the men and women merely players; They have their exits and their entrances, And one man in his time plays many parts, His acts being seven ages." *As You Like It*	In one of his most famous passages, Shakespeare again uses the metaphor of the theater to reflect how meaningless and unreal life can seem sometimes. Birth and death (exits and entrances) are inevitable, and every man who dies of old age experiences the same things – from infancy through to a second infancy (senility).

FAMOUS SHAKESPEARE QUOTATIONS
TEACHERS' VERSION
ANSWER: (PAGE 12)

WISE WORDS	YOUR INTERPRETATION:
"All that glisters is not gold." *The Merchant of Venice*	Just because something looks good doesn't necessarily mean it is (and vice-versa). Things are not always as they seem, whether this might be by accident or by someone employing deliberate deception.
"The course of true love never did run smooth;" *A Midsummer Night's Dream*	A line that will be of great comfort to arguing couples! Everyone has ups and downs in relationships, and just because things might get a bit "bumpy" doesn't mean you should necessarily stop the journey! Trouble is inevitable even in relationships defined by "true love."
"Cowards die many times before their deaths, The valiant never taste of death but once." *Julius Caesar*	Caesar says that brave men don't really think about their own deaths. It is inevitable anyway and foolish to waste time considering. Therefore, these brave men (like him!) only experience ("taste") death once – when it actually happens. Cowards fear death and dwell upon it, metaphorically dying "many times."
"Why then the world's mine oyster, Which I with sword will open." *The Merry Wives of Windsor*	In the play, Pistol is actually threatening Falstaff with taking his money by force. This meaning has long been forgotten and when people now say, "The world is my oyster," they mean they have a lot of great opportunities to experience ("open"), and it is up to them when they experience them. Everything is under their control. An oyster, after all, can contain a big, precious pearl!
"The first thing we do, let's kill all the lawyers." *Henry VI*	A very minor character, Dick the butcher, says this line which has come to sum up the general public's attitude towards bureaucrats who seem to just shuffle paper, upset people and charge an unjustified fortune for their "services." This might be unfair, but it's a popular quote!
"Once more unto the breach, dear friends, once more; Or close the wall up with our English dead. In peace there's nothing so becomes a man As modest stillness and humility; But when the blast of war blows in our ears, Then imitate the action of the tiger...." *Henry V*	Used by patriots across England, King Henry is encouraging his army (note how he encourages their loyalty by calling them "dear friends") to fight hard against the French. Although men should be still and humble in peaceful times, they should become tigers in times of war.

QUESTIONS – ACT ONE
TEACHERS' VERSION

ANSWER: (PAGE 18)

COSY CAPULETS

1.	**Which of the servants bites his thumb? (Scene 1)** Sampson
2.	**How old is Juliet? (Scene 2)** 13 (almost 14…but 14 is wrong!)
3.	**Whom does Lady Capulet want Juliet to marry? (Scene 3)** Paris
4.	**Who is Queen Mab? (Scene 4)** The fairies' midwife, as outlined by Mercutio
5.	**How many times do Romeo and Juliet kiss? (Scene 5)** Twice, in the playscript. Some film versions have more, some less.

MIND-BENDING MONTAGUES

1.	**How does Shakespeare immediately introduce Tybalt as a menacing character? Look closely at the language. (Scene 1)** The first word he says in the play is "What," which is instantly confrontational, and he even insults the other men, calling them "heartless hinds." He immediately challenges Benvolio, threatening him with "death." "What" is repeated, and he then says "hate" twice and calls Benvolio a coward – before launching into violence.
2.	**How does Shakespeare create an immediate mood of sadness around Romeo? Again, look closely at the language. (Scene 1)** Romeo asks basic questions which reflect his confused state of mind. He even seems unaware it is still morning, showing time is going slowly for him because his thoughts weigh heavily on his mind. He then admits he is lovesick. Even though there has been a big disturbance, Romeo doesn't immediately notice the damage caused, emphasizing his distracted mood.
3.	**How does Paris try to convince Capulet that Juliet isn't too young to be married? Were you surprised by this? (Scene 2)** When Paris is told Juliet is not quite fourteen, he responds "Younger than she are happy mothers made," meaning not only are some girls married at her age, but some are already bringing up children. Before people read the play, they often assume Juliet is age 16 or above. The culture was very different back then.
4.	**Explain why the Nurse and Juliet have a particularly close relationship. (Scene 3)** The Nurse rattles through several anecdotes about Juliet growing up – something her mother never does. She obviously loves Juliet a great deal and has fond memories. In fact, in many ways she is more of a mother to Juliet than Lady Capulet is. The Nurse breastfed her, as she too had a baby at the same time (who died).
5.	**Why do you think Shakespeare chose to have Romeo and Juliet use religious vocabulary when they first meet? (Scene 5)** Religion was an incredibly serious subject in the late sixteenth-century, much more important than it is today. By using words such as "shrine," "pilgrim" and "saints," Shakespeare (and Romeo, who begins this) raises the status of the pair's meeting, showing how important it is to both of them – and the rest of the play.

QUESTIONS – ACT TWO
TEACHERS' VERSION

ANSWER: (PAGE 19)

COSY CAPULETS	
1.	**The word "balcony" is mentioned nowhere in this scene. Why do you think it has become known as "The Balcony Scene"? (Scene 2)** "Juliet appears aloft as at a window" is the stage direction, so a balcony is often added.
2.	**With whom does Friar Laurence think Romeo has been spending time? (Scene 3)** Rosaline.
3.	**Romeo tells the Nurse the marriage arrangements. Where should Juliet go, and when? (Scene 4)** To Friar Laurence's cell, that afternoon (Monday…the day after they first met!).
4.	**The Nurse left Juliet at 9 o'clock. What time does she return with the message? (Scene 5)** She said she'd be half an hour, but it has taken her three hours – 12 o'clock.
5.	**What excuse is Juliet going to invent in order to get out of her house? (Scene 5)** That she has to go to "shrift" – confession.

MIND-BENDING MONTAGUES	
1.	**Why is Romeo's description of Juliet as "the sun" a particularly good metaphor? (Scene 2)** Lots of reasons. The sun is the giver of life to us and, more basically, gives us a pleasant feeling of warmth and enjoyment. It is also the center of our solar system, as Juliet is now to Romeo. Additionally, she "lights up his life." You can see how this can go on!
2.	**Why does Juliet not want Romeo to swear by the moon? (Scene 2)** The shape of the moon changes all the time (as we view it). It is a symbol of being inconstant and therefore unreliable. One could also say that it is associated with darkness and all the things that go with it (mystery, witchcraft, etc.)
3.	**Why does Friar Laurence agree to marry Romeo and Juliet? What do you think of his idea? (Scene 3)** He says, "For this alliance may so happy prove/To turn your households' rancour to pure love." He believes the marriage will bring the warring families together in peace. Reaction to his idea depends on individual opinion, but considering the depth of hatred between the families, Friar Laurence does appear to be incredibly naive or, at best, optimistic.
4.	**How is Tybalt's character developed in Scene 4…even though he isn't in it?** We discover that Tybalt has sent a letter to Romeo's house, challenging him to a fight. Mercutio, at some length, describes Tybalt as an expert in the art of duelling. Mercutio says he has all the latest (Italian) techniques of swordsmanship.
5.	**Explain how the Nurse, on her return from seeing Romeo, annoys Juliet. (Scene 5)** The Nurse has already taken two and a half hours longer than she said she would. Juliet is anxious to hear the message from Romeo, but the Nurse spins it out, talking about how tired she is, giving her opinion of Romeo, and then asking about Juliet's mother. When Juliet becomes angry, the Nurse tells her that she can run her own errands in future. Finally, she gives her the message!

QUESTIONS – ACT THREE
TEACHERS' VERSION

ANSWER: (PAGE 20)

COSY CAPULETS

1.	**What does Mercutio tease Benvolio about? (Scene 1)**
	His violent temper – which, of course, he doesn't have!
2.	**Why does Mercutio fight with Tybalt? (Scene 1)**
	Because Romeo won't and Tybalt has dishonored his friends.
3.	**At first, who does Juliet think has been killed when she meets the Nurse? (Scene 2)**
	Romeo.
4.	**What does Capulet change his mind about in Scene 4?**
	Paris marrying Juliet.
5.	**Where is Romeo going, after he leaves Juliet? (Scene 5)**
	Mantua (a nearby town).

MIND-BENDING MONTAGUES

1.	**Does Benvolio tell the truth in his account of the fighting? Explain your answer. (Scene 1)**
	Yes, in general, he is very truthful. He explains that Tybalt started the fight and Romeo killed him. He says Romeo spoke fairly to Tybalt. He says that Mercutio was just as angry as Tybalt; they fought, and Romeo tried to stop them, but Tybalt stabbed Mercutio from under Romeo's arm and fled. Romeo went for revenge, killed Tybalt, and ran away. The one thing he forgets to say is that he (Benvolio) told Romeo to run away!
2.	**Explain why Romeo thinks banishment is a punishment worse than death. (Scene 3)**
	He says, "There is no world without Verona walls" – this means his entire world (Juliet) is there and he isn't. Cats, dogs and even flies can see and touch her, but he cannot.
3.	**Why should Romeo be happy, according to Friar Laurence? (Scene 3)**
	Juliet is alive. Tybalt tried to kill Romeo but didn't succeed. Romeo's punishment for killing Tybalt should have been death, but he has only been banished. Romeo is still alive - and where there's life, there's hope.
4.	**In Scene 4, Capulet tells Paris he only wants a small wedding ceremony. Why?**
	People might think that the family is taking the very recent death of Tybalt far too lightly.
5.	**Explain Romeo and Juliet's reference to larks and nightingales. (Scene 5)**
	Juliet tells Romeo that the birdsong they can hear is that of the nightingale. Nightingales sing at night so, if true, this would mean that Romeo could stay for longer. Romeo knows it was the lark they heard, "the herald of the morn" and he has to leave Verona "or stay and die."

QUESTIONS – ACT FOUR
TEACHERS' VERSION
ANSWER: (PAGE 21)

	COSY CAPULETS
1.	**What does Paris call Juliet, which she objects to? (Scene 1)** His wife.
2.	**If the potion works as Friar Laurence hopes, for how long will Juliet be unconscious? (Scene 1)** 42 hours ("two and forty hours").
3.	**Why does Juliet want to get the Nurse and her mother out of her room? (Scene 3)** So she can take the potion.
4.	**When Juliet is found dead in her room on the morning of her wedding day, whom does Capulet say she has married? (Scene 5)** Death.
5.	**How does Friar Laurence try to reassure the Capulet family? (Scene 5)** By saying that Juliet is finally happy now and has gone to a better place. Those in the room think that he is referring to Heaven, but in fact he is referencing that she can now be with Romeo and "be in {her} Heaven."

	MIND-BENDING MONTAGUES
1.	**How does Juliet's conversation with Paris reveal a new dimension to her character? (Scene 1)** She seems more knowing, experienced and determined in this conversation – as if she has suddenly matured. The short lines reflect that she doesn't really want to speak to him at all; her individual responses are rather cool, and she eventually almost dismisses him by turning and talking to Friar Laurence.
2.	**Work through Friar Laurence's plan, step-by-step. Do you think it is a good plan? Explain your answer. (Scene 1)** Go home and agree to marry Paris. On Wednesday night, make sure you sleep on your own. Drink the potion, which will make you appear to be dead. You'll be taken to the Capulets' vault. I will write to Romeo to inform him of the plan. Romeo will return and collect you. Whatever you think…there's a lot that can go wrong with this plan!
3.	**Juliet explains her fears in Scene 3. What are they?** What if the potion doesn't work and she has to marry Paris? What if the Friar has given her poison so that his part in their marriage isn't revealed? What if she wakes before Romeo comes to get her – she might either suffocate or go insane by being surrounded by ghosts and all the dead bodies. Her insanity might even make her kill herself.
4.	**List some simple language techniques that Shakespeare uses to emphasize the shock and grief the characters feel at Juliet's "death." (Scene 4)** There is an incredible amount of exclamation marks, reflecting panic, volume and confusion. "O" is repeated many time too, signifying a simple verbal expression of pain and anguish. Lots of words are also repeated to show panic: "Help! Help!...Look, look!...She's dead, she's dead, she's dead!"
5.	**What is your reaction to Friar Laurence's speech, which begins "Peace ho, for shame!" (Hint – think of "dramatic irony"). (Scene 5)** It depends how it's delivered of course, but perhaps we feel that he does quite a good job here. Obviously we can detach ourselves from the grief of the Capulets because we, like the Friar, know the truth! He talks in terms of her being well and happy now in her new life. This is a double meaning of Heaven and with Romeo - indeed for her to be with Romeo is her idea of Heaven.

QUESTIONS – ACT FIVE
TEACHERS' VERSION

ANSWER: (PAGE 22)

COSY CAPULETS	
1.	**Why has Balthasar traveled to Mantua? (Scene 1)** To tell Romeo that Juliet is "dead" – he has seen her laid to rest.
2.	**How does Romeo persuade the Apothecary to sell him some poison? (Scene 1)** By appealing to his poverty. The law the Apothecary respects has not helped him.
3.	**What critical piece of news does Friar Laurence hear from Friar John? (Scene 2)** Laurence's letter to Romeo was not delivered.
4.	**When Romeo looks at the "dead" Juliet, what surprises him? (Scene 3)** Her beauty still remains. She doesn't seem to be dead (which of course she isn't!).
5.	**The Prince says that he himself has lost two kinsmen. To whom is he referring? (Scene 3)** Mercutio and Paris (both were relatives of the Prince, and neither belonged to the feuding families).

MIND-BENDING MONTAGUES	
1.	**What conclusion do you think Romeo has reached when he says, "Is it e'en so? then I defy you, stars!" (Scene 1)** Romeo says these words when he is told Juliet is dead. This links with his words after killing Tybalt, "O, I am fortune's fool!" Romeo feels he has been a plaything of fate and is now going to defy it, taking matters into his own hands – by killing himself and being reunited with Juliet in death.
2.	**Why is it important to the plot that Romeo uses a very strong poison, one which "if you had the strength/Of twenty men, it would dispatch you straight"? (Scene 1)** It completely removes the chance of any recovery or rescue for Romeo. As soon as he drinks it, he is as good as dead. It also works quickly, speeding up the action in the final scene.
3.	**Do you have sympathy for Paris? Explain your answer. (Scene 3)** Paris is a character who very much splits opinion in the play. Some find him an inconsequential distraction who provokes no other feelings but annoyance; others believe he is a good natured character who has always conducted himself well and didn't deserve his fate. Some reference to the text is necessary for a decent response.
4.	**One of the biggest examples of dramatic irony in the whole of Shakespeare's works is when Romeo says, "Death, that hath suck'd the honey of thy breath,/Hath had no power yet upon thy beauty:/Thou art not conquer'd." Explain the dramatic irony. How did you feel as a reader/audience member at this point? (Scene 3)** The reason Romeo is saying these things – quite correctly – is that Friar Laurence's potion is wearing off, blood is coming back to Juliet's lips and cheeks; she is about to awaken. Had Romeo arrived literally one minute later or Juliet awoken a minute earlier, the tragedy would have been avoided. It is not unknown for less controlled audience members to even shout out at this point!
5.	**Do you agree with Prince Escalus' conclusion that "All are punish'd"? Explain your views. (Scene 3)** Again, this is down to personal interpretation, but it is hard to find a major character in the play who has not suffered loss of some kind – all of it completely unnecessary.

SEQUENCING I
TEACHERS' VERSION

SOLUTION: (PAGE 23)

THE PROLOGUE

5   Two households, both alike in dignity,
     In fair Verona, where we lay our scene,

1   From ancient grudge break to new mutiny,
     Where civil blood makes civil hands unclean.

6   From forth the fatal loins of these two foes
     A pair of star-cross'd lovers take their life;

2   Whose misadventur'd piteous overthrows
     Doth with their death bury their parents' strife.

7   The fearful passage of their death-mark'd love,
     And the continuance of their parents' rage,

4   Which, but their children's end, nought could remove,
     Is now the two hours' traffic of our stage;

3   The which if you with patient ears attend,
     What here shall miss, our toil shall strive to mend.

SEQUENCING 1
TEACHERS' VERSION

SUGGESTED ANSWER: (PAGE 24)

UPDATE THE PROLOGUE

TASK:

Your task is to move the language forward 400 years or so and write a modern Prologue that gives all the information Shakespeare wanted the audience to have. And no – it doesn't have to have a rhyming scheme!

Teachers – try this yourself – it isn't easy! The modern version is only a suggested one, taken from the Plain Text version of Classical Comics' Graphic Novel.

Shakespeare's 16c. version	Your 21c. version
Two households, both alike in dignity, In fair Verona, where we lay our scene,	Two rich and powerful families Of Verona, where our story is set,
From ancient grudge break to new mutiny, Where civil blood makes civil hands unclean.	Re-start the feud between their houses, And once more, blood is shed.
From forth the fatal loins of these two foes A pair of star-cross'd lovers take their life;	One child from each side of this petty war Fall in love when they meet, when first they make sight.
Whose misadventur'd piteous overthrows Doth with their death bury their parents' strife.	And although their joy can never be, Their death brings peace and ends the fight.
The fearful passage of their death-mark'd love, And the continuance of their parents' rage,	The story of their doomed romance, The many killings in this affray,
Which, but their children's end, nought could remove, Is now the two hours' traffic of our stage;	How only their deaths could end violence Will be the subject of our tragic play.
The which if you with patient ears attend; What here shall miss, our toil shall strive to mend.	We'll take the time your patience now affords To fill the gaps left by these first few words.

SEQUENCING II
TEACHERS' VERSION

ANSWER: (PAGES 25-26)

THE PLAY – THIS ONE'S TOUGHER THAN TYBALT!

✂--

16.   Capulets and Montagues openly fight in a public place, though Romeo isn't present.

12.   Romeo tells Benvolio he is lovesick.

40.   Paris asks Capulet if he can marry Juliet, but he is refused.

4.   Lady Capulet tells Juliet that Paris wants to marry her.

33.   Romeo and Juliet meet at a party held at the Capulet house.

10.   Romeo and Juliet kiss for the first time.

21.   Romeo and Juliet discover they are from rival families.

18.   Romeo sneaks into the Capulet orchard to see Juliet.

3.   Romeo and Juliet decide to get married.

26.   Friar Laurence agrees to marry Romeo and Juliet.

24.   Mercutio and Benvolio discuss Tybalt and his challenge to Romeo.

29.   The Nurse gets a message from Romeo, telling Juliet when the marriage will be.

35.   Romeo and Juliet are married.

8.   Tybalt kills Mercutio.

37.   Romeo kills Tybalt.

1.   Romeo is banished from Verona by Prince Escalus.

34.   Hiding in Friar Laurence's cell, Romeo is stopped from stabbing himself.

27.   Capulet accepts Paris's offer to marry Juliet.

17.   The wedding night of Romeo and Juliet.

11.   Romeo leaves Verona to go to Mantua.

SEQUENCING II
TEACHERS' VERSION

ANSWER: (PAGES 25-26)

THE PLAY – THIS ONE'S TOUGHER THAN TYBALT!

✂ - - - - - - -

7.   Juliet is told she has to marry Paris.

31.   Juliet seeks the help of both her mother and the Nurse, but she is rejected.

23.   Paris and Juliet have an awkward conversation.

32.   Friar Laurence reveals a plan to help Juliet.

5.   Juliet drinks a potion that will give her death-like symptoms.

39.   Juliet is discovered "dead" in her chamber and taken to the Capulets' tomb.

25.   Balthasar visits Romeo in Mantua.

13.   Romeo buys some very strong poison from an Apothecary.

38.   Friar John tells Friar Laurence that he failed to deliver his letter to Romeo.

2.   Paris visits the Capulets' tomb.

19.   Romeo kills Paris.

36.   Romeo drinks the poison, kisses Juliet and dies.

9.   Friar Laurence enters the Capulets' tomb.

22.   Juliet wakes up from her unconscious state.

28.   Friar Laurence leaves the Capulets' tomb.

20.   Juliet kills herself with Romeo's dagger.

14.   Lord Montague says that his wife, Romeo's mother, has died of grief because of her son's his exile.

6.   Friar Laurence explains everything to Prince Escalus.

30.   Prince Escalus is angry with Capulet and Montague and says, "All are punish'd."

15.   Capulet and Montague shake hands and agree to build statues of their children.

WHAT HAPPENS NEXT?
TEACHERS' VERSION

ANSWER: (PAGES 30-33)

Comic Card	WHAT IS HAPPENING?
CARD 1	Tybalt refuses to listen to Benvolio's request to help him stop the fighting. Tybalt attacks Benvolio, and a riot breaks out between the Capulet and Montague families on Verona's streets.
CARD 2	Romeo has sneaked into Capulet's orchard and is listening to Juliet speaking to herself from her window. He then reveals his presence, and the pair have a long conversation, which ends with them planning to marry.
CARD 3	Romeo steps in between Tybalt and Mercutio. Tybalt then stabs Mercutio with his sword, giving him a fatal wound. Romeo goes after Tybalt, looking for revenge, and kills him, triggering the domino effect of tragic events, which eventually leads to the play's conclusion.
CARD 4	The Nurse goes to wake Juliet on the morning of her planned wedding to Paris. The Nurse discovers Juliet is "dead." The Capulet family and Paris mourn, and Juliet is taken to the Capulet tomb.

MATCHING QUOTATIONS
TEACHERS' VERSION

ANSWER: (PAGES 46 - 47)

Younger than she are happy mothers made.	**Paris**
I pray thee, good Mercutio, let's retire: The day is hot, the Capulets abroad, And, if we meet, we shall not 'scape a brawl;	**Benvolio**
From ancient grudge break to new mutiny, Where civil blood makes civil hands unclean.	**Chorus (Prologue)**
Romeo slew Tybalt, Romeo must not live.	**Lady Capulet**
This, by his voice, should be a Montague. Fetch me my rapier, boy.	**Tybalt**
O calm, dishonourable, vile submission!	**Mercutio**

MATCHING QUOTATIONS
TEACHERS' VERSION

ANSWER: (PAGES 46 - 47)

Younger than she are happy mothers made.	**Romeo**
I pray thee, good Mercutio, let's retire: The day is hot, the Capulets abroad, And, if we meet, we shall not 'scape a brawl;	**Friar Laurence**
From ancient grudge break to new mutiny, Where civil blood makes civil hands unclean.	**Juliet**
Romeo slew Tybalt, Romeo must not live.	**Prince Escalus**
This, by his voice, should be a Montague. Fetch me my rapier, boy.	**Nurse**
O calm, dishonourable, vile submission!	**Capulet**

CHARACTERS AND ADJECTIVES
TEACHERS' VERSION

ANSWER: (PAGE 48)

Not only does this task allow flexibility from students, it also creates much opportunity for discussion (not to mention the work on the basic skills of literary analysis, as particularly encouraged by the extension task).

What will quickly become obvious is that several characters have both negative and positive qualities when considered across the whole play. This should not be surprising – I mean, we're all a little like that, aren't we?

Also, some characters exhibit parts of one quality but blatantly don't embody it entirely – such as the Nurse and "understanding."

Some exhibit directly contrary qualities. With Tybalt, for example, one might be able to argue that he is strong in the physical sense, but weak mentally – bullies and violent people often are.
Or Prince Escalus, who could be considered strong in his pronouncements (or in his resistance to Lady Capulet's demands to have Romeo put to death), but considers himself weak in the end.

A word like "naive" is particularly good for discussion. For a start, depending on the group of students you have, the word itself might already be extending their vocabulary. But do students consider both Romeo and Juliet to be naive, or will they defend the purity and sincerity of their feelings and actions? Was Friar Laurence naive to think his plan would work? Was Lord Capulet naive to believe his suddenly headstrong daughter would obey him completely?

As you know, all of this is subjective (i.e. these are not "the answers"!), but here are some lists in which the adjectives applied could be readily justified:

Friar Laurence

forgiving	weak
kind	loving
clever	foolish
helpful	naive
understanding	optimistic

Romeo

headstrong	honorable	romantic
charming	loyal	spirited
weak	foolish	
strong	naive	
loving	optimistic	

Juliet

headstrong	strong	romantic
demanding	loving	spirited
forgiving	loyal	lively
temperamental	foolish	
resilient	naive	

Prince Escalus

demanding	strong
forgiving	intimidating
kind	threatening
understanding	weak

Nurse

headstrong	talkative	optimistic
good-humored	loving	practical
kind	loyal	romantic
helpful	foolish	
understanding	naive	

Lord Capulet

headstrong	vicious	honorable
good-humored	strong	threatening
demanding	nasty	foolish
forgiving	loving	naive
temperamental	intimidating	spirited & scary

Lady Capulet

nasty	loyal
loving	practical
cold	

Mercutio

headstrong	witty	loving
good-humored	clever	honorable
demanding	temperamental	loyal
charming	talkative	lively

Tybalt

headstrong	strong	scary
demanding	nasty	foolish
weak	intimidating	
temperamental	threatening	
vicious	spirited	

Benvolio

kind	loyal
helpful	practical
understanding	respectful
loving	
honorable	

Paris

charming	loyal
loving	romantic
honorable	respectful

ADJECTIVES – WIDENING YOUR VOCABULARY
TEACHERS' VERSION
ANSWER: (PAGE 49)

Here are some alternatives if you are suffering from a temporary mental block! (Of course, there are numerous nuances of meaning in many of these adjectives.) Depending on the results you get, it might be quite interesting (and amusing) to use this as the basis for further work on dialect/slang or standard and non-standard English.

Common adjective	Your alternative	Some from a thesaurus
good	great, smashing	wonderful, marvelous
nice	lovely, friendly	delightful, pleasing
bad	awful, poor	dire, terrible
happy	cheerful, pleased	ecstatic, joyful
excited	eager, moved	exhilarated, animated
hungry	peckish, starving	famished, ravenous
slow	steady, plodding	leisurely, sedate
quick	fast, nippy	nimble, swift
wet	soggy, soaking	drenched, saturated
hot	boiling, sweltering	sizzling, searing
dirty	filthy, foul	grimy, sullied
long	large, huge	imposing, monumental
old	elderly, ancient	aged, decrepit

95

METAPHORS
TEACHERS' VERSION
ANSWER: (PAGE 51)

Most teachers of English will have no problem filling in the middle column, but this has been supplied in case you want the metaphors within the context of the play. The references have been added to help you find the quotations, if necessary.

Shakespeare's metaphors	What is he describing?	Your metaphors
heartless hinds	This is Tybalt comparing the weaker servants to female deer – Act 1 Scene 1	
purple fountains issuing from your veins	blood pouring from wounds – Act 1 Scene 1	
golden window of the east	Benvolio describes the sunrise – Act 1 Scene 1	
love is a smoke made with the fume of sighs	Romeo is lovesick over Rosaline – Act 1 Scene 1	
I will make thee think they swan a crow	Benvolio is going to show Romeo some women at the party who are far better than Rosaline – Act 1 Scene 2	
He's a man of wax	The Nurse says Paris is a very handsome man, like a wax sculpture – Act 1 Scene 3	
I have a soul of lead	Romeo is depressed – Act 1 Scene 4	
dreams, which are the children of an idle brain	Mercutio reprimands Romeo for believing his dreams – Act 1 Scene 4	

METAPHORS
TEACHERS' VERSION
ANSWER: (PAGE 52)

Shakespeare's metaphors	What is he describing?	Your metaphors
a snowy dove trooping with crows	**Romeo sees Juliet; she stands out from the crowd – Act 1 Scene 5**	
my lips, two blushing pilgrims	**Romeo prepares to kiss Juliet; his lips are ready to pay pilgrimage to hers, blushing and red. – Act 1 Scene 5**	
Juliet is the sun	**Romeo sees Juliet "aloft as at a window" in the balcony scene; she lights the dark for him – Act 2 Scene 2**	
I have night's cloak to hide me	**Romeo will be safe, as he is hidden by the darkness – Act 2 Scene 2**	
I am fortune's fool	**Romeo feels like he is being used as a plaything of fate – Act 3 Scene 1**	
Come, civil night, thou sober-suited matron, all in black	**Juliet is looking forward to her wedding night, which looks plainly dressed in black (black of night) – Act 3 Scene 2**	
Night's candles are burnt out, and jocund day stands tiptoe on the misty mountain tops	**Romeo describes dawn breaking after his wedding night – Act 3 Scene 5**	
you slug-a-bed!	**The Nurse calls Juliet lazy as she won't get out of bed – we know she is "dead" – Act 4 Scene 5**	
Thou detestable maw (stomach), thou womb of death, gorg'd with the dearest morsel of the earth	**Romeo breaks into the Capulets' tomb, which he likens to a stomach from a creature that eats people – Act 5 Scene 3**	
winking at your discords	**Prince Escalus feels he has been "turning a blind eye" to the families' behavior – Act 5 Scene 3**	

OXYMORONS
TEACHERS' VERSION

SUGGESTED ANSWER: (PAGE 53)
The oxymorons have been set out like this to allow you to do some follow up tasks of your choice involving group work and the handing out of cards.

One drama-related idea is to randomly give one of the cards below to a pair or group and get them to do a frieze/tableau representing their oxymoron.

brawling love	loving hate	heavy lightness
serious vanity	bright smoke	cold fire
sick health	still-waking sleep	sweet sorrow
beautiful tyrant	fiend angelical	dove-feathered raven
wolvish-ravening lamb	damned saint	honorable villain

JULIET'S AMBIGUITY
TEACHERS' VERSION

ANSWER: (PAGE 54)

The lines	What Lady Capulet *thinks* Juliet means	What Juliet *really* means
no man like he doth grieve my heart.	Romeo has upset her because he killed Tybalt	Her heart is grieving over Romeo because he is banished.
Ay, madam, from the reach of these my hands: 'Would, none but I might venge my cousin's death!	Juliet is so keen on revenge, she wants to carry it out on Romeo personally.	Juliet doesn't want anyone other than herself to carry out the revenge (because she wants to protect him and would do nothing herself).
Indeed, I never shall be satisfied With Romeo, till I behold him – dead – Is my poor heart so for a kinsman vex'd.	Juliet will never be satisfied until she sees Romeo dead. Her heart is troubled because of what's happened to Tybalt.	The dashes are the key! She will never be satisfied until she sees Romeo again. Her poor heart is dead because of the trouble Romeo is in.
Madam, if you could find out but a man To bear a poison, I would temper it, That Romeo should, upon receipt thereof, Soon sleep in quiet.	Juliet wants to kill Romeo by giving him poison.	Juliet would mix the poison so weakly it would merely give him a restful night's sleep.
O! how my heart abhors To hear him nam'd, and cannot come to him, To wreak the love I bore my cousin Upon his body that hath slaughter'd him!	Juliet hates hearing Romeo's name without being able to get hold of him and punish him for what he has done to Tybalt.	Juliet hates hearing Romeo's name without being able to hold him – for romantic purposes!

MISSING WORDS
TEACHERS' VERSION

ANSWER: (PAGES 55)

The answers are below in **bold.**

1.   Juliet is **thirteen** years old in the play.

2.   The town Romeo goes to when he is exiled is **Mantua**.

3.   Mercutio is the Prince's **kinsman**.

4.   **Benvolio** has a reputation of being a peace maker.

5.   "That which we call a **rose**,
       By any other word would smell as sweet;"

6.   Romeo and Juliet met on a **Sunday** and were married on the **Monday**.

7.   "O, I am fortune's **fool**."

8.   **Lady Montague** dies of grief at the end of the play.

9.   The person who informs Romeo of Juliet's death is **Balthasar**.

10.   "For never was a story of more **woe**,
       Than this of Juliet and her Romeo."

CLOSE TEXTUAL ANALYSIS
TEACHERS' VERSION

ACT 2 SCENE 2: SUGGESTED ANSWER: (PAGE 57)

Of course, in any exercise of this nature, there will be many and varying interpretations of the lines. In fact, that is desirable. Below are some interpretations for you to consider.

1. He jests at scars that never felt a wound.
   In the previous scene, Mercutio was teasing Romeo about being lovesick. Here, Romeo is saying that it's easy to joke about something when you've never experienced what it feels like. The choice of metaphor Romeo uses is interesting as it reflects the pain a spurned lover feels.

2. But, soft! what light through yonder window breaks? It is the east, and Juliet is the sun!
   The actual light Romeo sees is far more mundane – it's the light coming from Juliet's bedroom. But, as is his wont, he turns something simple into something romantic and describes the window as the east (where the sun rises) and Juliet as the sun. The sun is a simple but effective metaphor. Think of what role the sun plays to us – our world revolves around it, it warms us, it's bright, we can't live without it...

3. The brightness of her cheek would shame those stars, As daylight doth a lamp; her eyes in heaven, Would through the airy region stream so bright, That birds would sing and think it were not night.
   Continuing the theme of light (Juliet), Romeo talks about her physical beauty (which, after all, is what has attracted him in the first place). This is an example of hyperbole. He is so affected, she almost becomes a living goddess for him, capable of superhuman acts.

4. O Romeo, Romeo! wherefore art thou Romeo? Deny thy father, and refuse thy name; Or, if thou wilt not, be but sworn my love, And I'll no longer be a Capulet.
   The first line is perhaps the most misinterpreted in all of literature. Most people think it means "Where are you?" especially as Juliet is at a window gazing out into the orchard. It actually means "Why are you Romeo?" or, more to the point, "Why do you have to be a Montague?" She asks Romeo to cast off his family ties and his name so that she and Romeo can be together. However, if he will not, she is prepared to cut her Capulet ties.

5. What's in a name? That which we call a rose, By any other word would smell as sweet;
   An example of Shakespeare's genius for encapsulating vast, difficult philosophical concepts in a simple, memorable phrase. Juliet distinguishes things (in this case a rose...but meaning Romeo Montague, too) from the label that is attached to them. Juliet feels the thing itself is most important, not the name arbitrarily given to it.

6. My ears have yet not drunk a hundred words Of thy tongue's uttering, yet I know the sound.
   Shakespeare reminds us how impulsive the pair are being here. Juliet frankly admits she hardly knows him by saying she hasn't even heard him speak a hundred words (to be pedantic, it's a few more by the time she's said this, but not many...it was only 90 words at the party!). The last part reinforces how Romeo's few words have had a great impact on her, as she already recognizes his voice.

7. (Juliet) If they do see thee, they will murder thee. (Romeo) Alack! there lies more peril in thine eye Than twenty of their swords: look thou but sweet, And I am proof against their enmity.
   Another example of hyperbole; yet this is not an unusual feeling for a young man who feels like everything is right in the world. Adrenaline and his beating heart make Romeo feel invincible. It's a reflection of the power Juliet now unwittingly has over Romeo – she can hurt him more than swords (even twenty of them!).

8. O gentle Romeo! If thou dost love, pronounce it faithfully; Or if thou think'st I am too quickly won, I'll frown, and be perverse, and say thee nay, So thou wilt woo; but, else, not for the world.
   Juliet realizes she hasn't been very good in taking the usual female role in a traditional courtship. A young woman would certainly be expected to make Romeo work a bit harder for her companionship than she has done! So she says that if Romeo feels she has been too "easily won," she will pretend she doesn't really like him and refuse his advances... but only so he will come back and court her more – not for any other reason (i.e. she really does like him!).

9. Do not swear at all; Or, if thou wilt, swear by thy gracious self, Which is the god of my idolatry, And I'll believe thee.
   Romeo wants to "swear" to prove the depth of his feelings for Juliet and tries to swear by the moon. Juliet tells him not to - but if he is compelled to swear, he should do so by himself because he has become a god in her eyes. Therefore, that would be swearing by something very worthwhile and serious (unlike the moon), and she would believe him. More hyperbole!

10. O blessed, blessed night! I am afeard, Being in night, all this is but a dream, Too flattering-sweet to be substantial.
    Of course, it is night time and that is when dreams usually happen. Romeo gets the feeling that things are going so well, he must be imagining them. He isn't used to this (this never happened with Rosaline). The repetition of "blessed," another example of religious vocabulary hanging over from Act 1 Scene 5, emphasizes the high level of his emotions.

FORMAL DEBATE
TEACHERS' VERSION

NOTES FOR TEACHERS: (PAGES 58 - 59)

This activity, on the face of it, might seem a little imposing. It isn't, honestly! What you have is a step-by-step guide for students (and teachers) on how to conduct one version of a formal debate.

I say "one version" because there are many variations on the theme of formal debates – the number of speakers can change, and other people will use different terminology.

I have done this activity many, many times, and, like any other lesson, it is not a guaranteed success – but even with very low ability students, if you get the right "motion" you can have a very animated speaking and listening task on your hands.

SOME TIPS:

- Some time before you want to have the debate, agree on a motion and take volunteers for the roles of speakers and Chair. Unless your students are very gifted, the speakers will need homework time to prepare. Give them a time limit for their speeches. Unless they are very good speakers (depending on their age), five minutes is often enough. You can leave it open-ended if you want to take the risk!

- Guide the speakers in what they need to do. They should work together (either inside or outside of class, depending on logistics) to come up with a set of points that they can turn into sentences, then paragraphs, then a speech. They need to work together so they aren't duplicating each other's points, and it will also help if they can do some research together

- Insist on the formality, if possible. Students usually respond positively to it.

- If you are doing this for the first time, you might want to act as Chair. It can be a challenging role, but if you choose a willing student, you will always be there to help and intervene if necessary. It makes for great personal development for the Chair if you can resist intervening until it's absolutely unavoidable. Discuss with or inform the Chair of the time limits and help him or her keep to them.

- Lead the applause for each speech!

- When the Chair takes questions from the floor, get him or her to write a list of those wanting to contribute, as this is more equitable and saves students from having to keep their arms raised. People who want to contribute can raise their hands, and the Chair can add them to the list.

- When voting, it's often a good idea for the speakers to turn around to save any embarrassment or influence. You may wish to consider a written vote instead.

ESSAY WRITING
TEACHERS' VERSION

NOTES FOR TEACHERS: (PAGE 74 - 75)

If you have a reasonably able class, the suggested essay title will produce responses that are far too long – for you and them! There are potentially many, many points to consider – especially in point 4 of the plan – which could turn out to be an analysis (linguistic, social, moral, philosophical!) of the whole "Balcony Scene."

The title can be tweaked by limiting the focus to a set of lines within the scenes or simply looking at Shakespeare's treatment of violence OR love in just one of the scenes (or a section of the relevant scene).

If you have a less able group, the wide ranging scope of the title suggested should provide them with plenty of writing opportunities.

Regardless of their ability, you will need to offer support to students in directing them to important lines as well as explaining the significance of some of the language.

The essay title and plan can be amended for younger students.

Point 5 of the plan provides ample opportunity for the students to realize that it is their opinion that matters, and the beauty of English and English Literature is that two people with directly contradictory opinions can both earn the highest grades.

ROMEO AND JULIET SPELLING JUMBLE
TEACHERS' VERSION

SOLUTION: (PAGE 76)

Jumbled Spelling	Correct Spelling
NICE PR	PRINCE
ORE VAN	VERONA
MORGUE NAME TOO	ROMEO MONTAGUE
PLACATE DULY	LADY CAPULET
A FUNERAL CRIER	FRIAR LAURENCE
A TROPHY ACE	APOTHECARY
OUT CRIME	MERCUTIO
AUNT MA	MANTUA
POOR GLUE	PROLOGUE
ENSCONCE ABLY	BALCONY SCENE
LETTUCE JAIL UP	JULIET CAPULET
HARDLINE'US PAL	ALL ARE PUNISH'D

ROMEO AND JULIET WORD SEARCH
TEACHERS' VERSION

SOLUTION: (PAGE 77)

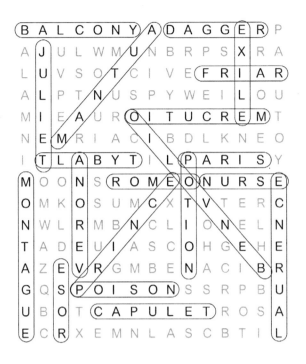

ROMEO
VERONA
POISON
CAPULET
MERCUTIO
NURSE
FRIAR
DAGGER
BALCONY
EXILE

JULIET
PRINCE
BENVOLIO
MONTAGUE
TYBALT
POTION
LAURENCE
ROSE
PARIS
MANTUA

ROMEO AND JULIET CROSSWORD
TEACHERS' VERSION

SOLUTION: (PAGE 78)

Across

1 STRATFORD
3 MANTUA
5 VERONA
6 JULIET
9 MONTAGUE
11 ANGRY
13 TOMB
16 PRINCE
18 DAGGER
21 PETER
24 GLOBE
25 EXILE
28 BALTHASAR

Down

1 SHAKESPEARE
2 ROSALINE
4 THIRTEEN
7 TYBALT
8 CAPULET
10 MAB
12 GOLD
14 MOON
15 ROPE
16 PLAGUE
17 NURSE
19 GHOST
20 ROMEO
21 PARIS
22 ROSE
23 FRIAR
26 EAST
27 POISON

COMIC PAGE GRID